Serverless GraphQL APIs with Amazon's AWS AppSync

Matthias Biehl

First edition: May 2018

Biehl, Matthias
      API-University Press
      Volume 8 of the API-University Series.
      Includes illustrations, bibliographical references and index.
      ISBN-13: 978-1717110701
      ISBN-10: 1717110703

API-University Press
https://www.api-university.com
info@api-university.com

Contents

Abstract

This book gets you a running start with serverless GraphQL APIs on Amazon's AWS AppSync. GraphQL is now a viable option for modern API design. And since Facebook, Yelp, and Shopify have built successful APIs with GraphQL, many companies consider following in the technological footsteps of these tech giants. Using GraphQL is great, but by itself, it is only half the rent: It requires the manual installation and maintenance of software infrastructure components.

AppSync is a cloud-based platform for GraphQL APIs. It is serverless, so you waste no time setting up infrastructure. It scales up and down dynamically depending on the load. It supports your app developers with an SDK for synchronization and offline support. You pay only what you use, so no upfront investment is needed and it may save your organizations thousands of dollars in IT costs.

Whether you are new to GraphQL, or you are an experienced GraphQL developer, this book will provide you with the knowledge needed to get started with AWS AppSync. After quickly covering the GraphQL foundations, you will dive into the practice of developing APIs with AWS AppSync with in-depth walkthroughs, screenshots, and code samples. The book guides you through the step-by-step process of creating a GraphQL schema, developing GraphQL APIs, connecting data sources, developing resolvers with AppSync templates, securing your API, offering real-time data, developing offline support and synchronization for your apps and much more.

1 Introduction to AppSync & GraphQL

1.1 What is an API?

Modern applications are typically *distributed systems*, consisting of a *frontend* and a *backend*. The frontend displays the user interface, with its icons, buttons, and graphics. It may be a website, a mobile app, or a voice-based app. The backend stores and delivers the business data. It is typically realized on an application server.

Frontend and backend run on different machines, but the data, which is managed by the backend systems, needs to be delivered to the frontend systems, where it is displayed. To manage the communication between frontend and backend, an API , short for *application programming interface*, is introduced. In this pattern, the backend serves the API, the frontend consumes the API. To realize this pattern, an API server needs to be built on the backend side and an API client is built on the frontend side.

But first, let's have a look at the interaction between frontend and backend. In which ways may the frontend interact with the backend? The frontend may

- retrieve data from the backend

- write new data to the backend or update data on the backend

- get notified by the backend, as soon as the data on the backend changes

These needs of frontends regarding the interaction with backends are quite universal. Thus, a couple of philosophies, such as RPC, SOAP, REST, and GraphQL, have been developed to structure the interaction between frontend and backend.

1.2 What is GraphQL?

In this book, we take a hands-on approach to learning GraphQL. We first explore the concepts of the two GraphQL languages using examples.

GraphQL allows us to build APIs for retrieving data, writing data and getting notified in real-time when data changes. GraphQL provides a new philosophy for building APIs, which helps us to structure the interaction between frontend and backend. To structure the interaction, GraphQL offers three things: a declarative, typed query language for APIs (see section 1.2.1), a schema language for specifying data structures (see section 1.2.2) and a runtime for building APIs (see section 1.2.3).

GraphQL was originally developed as proprietary technology by Facebook, but was open-sourced in 2015 and is now licensed under the Open Web Foundation Agreement (OWFa). The GraphQL specification is available in the form of a working draft [6].

1.2.1 GraphQL Query Language

GraphQL offers a *query language* for APIs. The language allows the frontend to interact with the backend. The language provides primitives for retrieving data, writing data and getting notified when data changes.

The GraphQL query language is *declarative*. Another well-known declarative query language is SQL, which is used for interacting with relational database servers. In a declarative language, we specify WHAT we want as a result, and not HOW the result should be computed. We let the server figure out HOW the result is computed. A declarative language provides an appropriate level of abstraction for clients. Clients can interact with the data, without having to worry about backend implementation details. The interaction is easy from the perspective of a client. The heavy lifting needs to be done on the server side.

1.2.2 GraphQL Schema Language

GraphQL allows us to define and describe our data structures. For this purpose, GraphQL provides a *typed schema language*. We specify custom types for the data served by the API. A GraphQL schema is created by defining types, which have a number of fields, and by providing access functions for each field and each type.

1.2.3 GraphQL Runtime

When implementing the API for our data schema, we use the generic GraphQL runtime. The GraphQL runtime provides an implementation of the common functionality that needs to be provided by all GraphQL APIs. Which features are those? GraphQL APIs have a single endpoint, which can receive and resolve GraphQL queries written in the GraphQL query language (see section 1.2.1). The data served on this endpoint conforms to the schema, which is written in the GraphQL schema language (see section 1.2.2).

By providing an implementation of the common functionality, the GraphQL runtime helps us to build APIs quickly. Nevertheless, the GraphQL runtime does not limit us too much in our implementation. GraphQL can be connected to any backend, such as a host system, a middleware, a SOAP web service, REST API, relational database or NoSQL database[1]. GraphQL

---

[1]There is no link between graph databases (such as Neo4j) and GraphQL.

15

is not tied to any specific database or storage engine.

1.2.4 A GraphQL Application

A GraphQL application consists of a GraphQL API, which is part of the backend, and a GraphQL client, which is part of the frontend. The GraphQL client sends GraphQL queries (see chapter 3.3) to the GraphQL API. The GraphQL API processes queries in the following way:

1. The API receives the request and extracts the query. The query may be bound to HTTP and encoded in a JSON data structure (see chapter 10.4).

2. The API checks and validates the query (see chapter 10.1) to ensure it only refers to the types and fields that are defined in the schema.

3. The API resolves the query to produce a result (see chapter 10.2). For this purpose, it may interact with backend systems and databases. The result is typically encoded in JSON and is sent back to the client.

1.3 What is AppSync?

AWS AppSync is a fully-managed serverless GraphQL infrastructure. Because it runs on a serverless, managed infrastructure, it scales automatically and does not require any manual installation nor any maintenance. Thus, AppSync allows us to get started quickly without any impediments. And right from the start, we can focus on creating functionality with business value.

1.3.1 AppSync Architecture

Let's have a look at the AppSync architecture. In Figure 1.1 we have depicted such a high-level solution architecture for an app, an AppSync API and AWS data sources. On the left-hand side we have the clients connecting to the API in the middle, and on the right-hand side we have the data sources feeding the API.

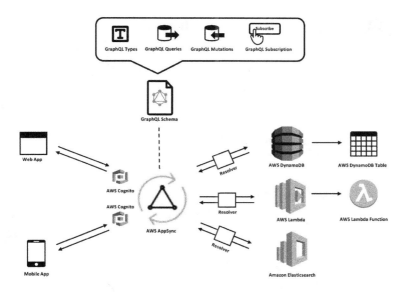

Figure 1.1: AppSync Architecture

The API is realized on the AppSync infrastructure, using GraphQL concepts, and it is secured using e.g. AWS Cognito. The API is defined by a GraphQL schema, consisting of types, queries, mutations, and subscriptions. The data of the API is delivered by any of the AWS data sources on the right: an Amazon DynamoDB, Amazon Elasticsearch or an AWS Lambda function. The raw data delivered by the data sources is transformed to GraphQL with a resolver.

1.3.1.1 AppSync Clients

AppSync clients (left side in Figure 1.1) use the GraphQL API. The clients interact with the API using the GraphQL query language. Learn more about creating AppSync clients in chapter 9 and about writing GraphQL queries, mutations, and subscriptions in section 3.3.

1.3.1.2 GraphQL Server and Schema

AWS AppSync has a powerful GraphQL server (in the middle of Figure 1.1), which is used by all APIs on AppSync. Each API supports the definition of custom types and the three GraphQL methods: query (read-only), mutation (write), and subscription (event-based notification). Learn more about GraphQL schema in section 3.2 and the use of GraphQL schema within AppSync in section 4.1.

1.3.1.3 Data Sources

The data served via a GraphQL API is usually in an existing database. AppSync offers a convenient way to connect databases from the AWS cloud:

- Amazon DynamoDB

- Amazon Elasticsearch

- Services deployed on AWS Lambda

Learn more about AppSync data sources in section 4.2.

1.3.1.4 Resolvers

Resolvers define a mapping from a GraphQL request to a data source request and from a data source response back to a GraphQL response. According to these two steps, the mapping consists of request mapping and a response mapping. Learn more about writing AppSync resolvers in section 5. Writing resolvers is the main software development activity when creating a GraphQL API. AppSync uses new concepts, a templating language and predefined templates to simplify resolver development. Learn more about AppSync resolver tooling in section 6.

1.3.2 App Sync Use Cases

1.3.2.1 Simple Data-Centric GraphQL API

A typical use-case for AppSync is providing a data-centric API to an existing data source. The advantage of AppSync is the simplicity of building such a GraphQL API, especially when connecting to Amazon Elasticsearch, AWS Lambda or Amazon DynamoDB. Not having to set up any infrastructure allows for quick turnaround times.

1.3.2.2 Offline Access and Synchronization for Apps

AppSync clients may add a local offline storage for the data delivered by the GraphQL API. This offline storage is a cache that works as follows: A copy of each query request and response is cached locally and for each mutation, the cache is updated with a write-through strategy, meaning the data is written both to the cache and to the GraphQL API.

Offline support allows us to create optimistic user interfaces, that provide a consistent user experience regardless of the current network availability. With an optimistic UI, data can be manipulated when the device is in an offline state.

Offline support is only a practical option, if the client is able to synchronize offline data back to the server when it comes online again. Server-side and client-side conflict resolution in addition to the synchronization mechanism are needed to support this use case. Both are provided by AppSync.

1.3.2.3 Data Merging and Unification

Data merging is a common use case for GraphQL APIs, and AppSync supports this use case with its technology stack. In AppSync we do not need to decide on a single data source per API. We can connect as many data sources as we want to an AppSync API, all at the same time. Thus, an AppSync API is ideal for data merging. The goals of data merging are:

- Connecting to multiple data sources, which can be databases, APIs, Lambda functions or Elasticsearch domains.

- Offering one common API, with one URL, on a common technology stack. Instead of having to navigate to various APIs on different URLs, which are each protected by their own security mechanism, the GraphQL API can offer all the data on one URL protected by a common security mechanism.

- Linking data from various data sources with each other, so we can navigate from the data provided by one data source to the data provided by another data source. In a database world, this would corresponds to joining data from separate tables together. But in our case, we use GraphQLand its resolvers to implement the joining logic.

To realize data merging functionality efficiently with AppSync, there are a couple of constraints:

- The resolver for any single field should only be connected to one data source. This ensures that we can use the App-Sync templates for writing resolvers.

- The data sources need to be AppSync compatible. Some data may be in an Amazon DynamoDB, other data may be in third-party software, accessible via API. To access the

20

third-party APIs, we first need to create an AWS Lambda function as a proxy for each third-party API. Via these proxies, we can integrate the third party-APIs with App-Sync.

1.3.3 Advantages

Writing APIs on the AppSync and GraphQL stack is more and more popular, as it provides a couple of advantages. Let's look at some of the advantages of using GraphQL (see section 1.3.3.1), the serverless infrastructure (see section 1.3.3.2) and the pricing model of the infrastructure (see section 1.3.3.3).

1.3.3.1 GraphQL

AppSync APIs are based on GraphQL and rely on the GraphQL engine for processing requests. GraphQL allows us to build a low latency APIs, which serve complex, high dimensional and big data sets. GraphQL allows us to merge responses sent to different backends. Using a single query, can we construct a nested response from multiple data sources. As a result, we can build an endpoint, which we can securely aggregate and paginate through.

GraphQL can be used as a convenient abstraction layer on top of already existing data sources and APIs. It is possible to hide the diverse APIs, microservices and database technologies of an enterprise behind a commonly designed and governed GraphQL API.

The selling features to a developer community are strong typing and the self-documenting contract between client and server. Developers can also use GraphQL features for data discovery without having knowledge of the backend data sources.

The GraphQL engine of AppSync is optimized and performs data loading in a batch for efficiency reasons. It can also manage conflict detection and resolution.

1.3.3.2 Serverless

GraphQL is great (see section 1.3.3.1), but requires the manual installation and maintenance of software infrastructure components, tedious configuration, and some manual tweaking. And when running a productive GraphQL system, you need to find a way to scale the system up and down based on the current load.

The advantages you gain from serverless GraphQL are:

- No server management (no need to install or manage any machine)

- No software management (no need to install or manage GraphQL servers)

- Pay-per-execution (never pay for idle)

- Auto-scale (scale based on demand)

AppSync allows us to focus on building apps and GraphQL APIs while minimizing the time spent and effort exerted on managing the infrastructure needed to run GraphQL. In AppSync, developers can work with their data via a GraphQL API. GraphQL can be easily integrated with modern tools and frameworks.

1.3.3.3 Pricing

I won't go into the exact numbers and prices, as they are subject to change, so check out the current prices on the AWS website. But it is important to understand the pricing model: what are the parameters, how do they contribute to the overall price and how do they grow?

With GraphQL we only pay for each query, mutation or subscription execution, and not for idle CPU time. AppSync will be charged based on the total number of operations and real-time updates:

- a couple of dollars per million query and mutation operations

- a couple of dollars per million real-time updates

- a couple of dollars per million minutes of connection for real-time updates.

- data transfer at the EC2 data transfer rate

- real-time updates are priced per payload delivered

2 AppSync Tutorial

In this tutorial, we will build our first AppSync API. We will work with the AppSync user interface, so lots of screenshots are provided for you to easily find your way around AWS AppSync.

In the following, we walk through all the steps that are required for development of a new API with AppSync:

- Get Started with AppSync (see section 2.1)

- Create an AppSync API (see section 2.2)

- Configure the API on the AppSync dashboard (see section 2.3)

- Define a Schema (see section 2.4)

- Connect Data Sources (see section 2.5)

- Map the Schema to Data Source via a Resolver (see section 2.6)

- Test and Access the API (see section 2.7)

- Build an App based on the API (see section 2.8)

2.1 Get Started

To use AppSync, you need to have an AWS account. If you do not have one yet, register for one, you might be eligible for the so-called free tier, allowing you to use several AWS services free of charge for a year.

To get started, let's open the AWS AppSync console. There are at least two ways to get there:

1. Open the AppSync Console directly and log in with your AWS account.

    - https://console.aws.amazon.com/appsync/home

2. Log in to the generic AWS console first, open the services menu and select *AWS AppSync* from the *Mobile Services* Category (see Figure 2.1). If *AWS AppSync* is not available, switch to another data center (upper right-hand corner) first, such as *US East (N. Virginia)*, and open the menu again.

    - https://console.aws.amazon.com

Figure 2.1: Select AppSync from the AWS Services Menu

We are now on the home screen of AWS AppSync. If we already had APIs, we could see an overview of the APIs here. Since we do not have an AppSync API yet, we can now start by creating our first API, as described in the next section.

2.2 Create API

Let's create a new GraphQL API. Click the *Create API* button on the AppSync home screen. A wizard for creating a new API appears, as shown in Figure 2.2. It asks as for two things: a name for the API and a schema

1. Let's give the API a name, such as *MyAppSync App* in our example.

2. A GraphQL API is defined by its schema, thus we have to define it when creating a new API. In this tutorial, we will work with the provided *sample schema*. Let's select it in the wizard. For future use cases, we could alternatively start by uploading an existing GraphQL schema. In any case, this is just an initial schema and we can edit it later on.

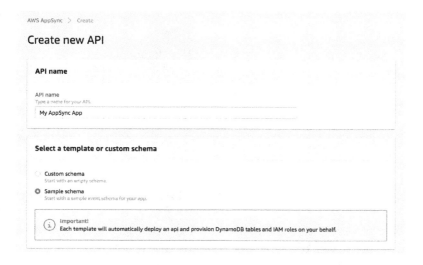

Figure 2.2: Create the first API

After selecting the sample schema option, you can scroll down to the sample schema shown in Figure 2.3. The sample schema defines GraphQL types for **Events** and **Comments**. Learn more about the *GraphQL Schema Language* in section 3.2.

Sample event schema

```
1   type Comment {
2       # The id of the comment's parent event.
3       eventId: ID!
4       # A unique identifier for the comment.
5       commentId: String!
6       # The comment's content.
7       content: String!
8       # The comment timestamp. This field is indexed to enable sorted pagination.
9       createdAt: String!
10  }
11
12  type CommentConnection {
13      items: [Comment]
14      nextToken: String
15  }
16
17  type Event {
18      id: ID!
19      name: String
20      where: String
21      when: String
22      description: String
23      # Paginate through all comments belonging to an individual post.
24      comments(limit: Int = 10, nextToken: String): CommentConnection
25  }
26
27  type EventConnection {
28      items: [Event]
29      nextToken: String
```

Figure 2.3: Sample GraphQL Schema Definition

Let's confirm our initial API configuration to create the API. The newly created API can already be used, however, it does not really do anything useful, yet. In the following steps, we configure the API so it behaves as needed.

2.3 Configure the API on the API Dashboard

After creating an API with the wizard, we get directed to the dashboard page of the newly created API. It is the starting point for configuring all the aspects of the GraphQL API, especially now, after it has been recently created. But also later, during development, we will return to this API dashboard to change aspects of the API.

So what information is on the dashboard? As shown in figure 2.4, the dashboard contains a navigation bar on the left-hand side and a detailed view on the right-hand side.

The navigation bar on the left lists all our AppSync APIs, and for the currently selected API it provides an overview of four API aspects: (1) schema definition, (2) testing with queries, (3) connected data sources and (4) some general settings.

On the right-hand side, the API dashboard provides some details of the API, such as its URL we can use to call it and the credentials (API key) required for calling the API.

Figure 2.4: AppSync Dashboard

Whenever we come back to this API to configure a certain aspect of it or to develop it further, we first go to this AppSync API dashboard.

Now, let's navigate in the left-hand navigation menu to the settings page (see Figure 2.5). On the settings page we can configure the authorization (more on security in chapter 8) and the logging to AWS Cloudwatch (more on logging in section 11.4).

Figure 2.5: Settings Page on the AppSync Dashboard

2.4 Define GraphQL Schema

Via the left-hand navigation, we can reach the schema page, which is depicted in Figure 2.6. On the schema page, we can edit and define the schema and attach resolvers to each type and each field. Since we have started with a pre-defined sample schema, the schema editor is already populated with this schema.

Figure 2.6: GraphQL Schema Definition

In the middle of the screen, we can see our schema in the

schema editor. The schema is defined using the GraphQL schema language, which we will study in depth in section 3.2. The schema editor provides a user-friendly interface with search and auto-complete capabilities. We also have the possibility to export the GraphQL schema, either in json or graphql format. The exported schema can be used in API clients (see section 2.8)

On the right side of the screen, we have a logical view of the schema, displaying the GraphQL types (e.g. `Comment`) and fields with their respective types (e.g. `eventID` of type ID). For each field, we can attach a resolver (see section 2.6 and chapter 5).

The button *Create Resources* on the top of the screen allows us to create a new database table based on a GraphQL type and it allows us to write getters and setters (a.k.a. queries and mutations) for the specified types. The first step is to define the object and how it is represented in the database, see Figure 2.7.

Figure 2.7: Creating a new Resource

So, once the type is defined in GraphQL, the getter, setter, and database table can be generated, instead of writing the respective code for the schema. In Figure 2.8 you can see the proposed generated getters and setters for adding a new `Comment` resource.

Figure 2.8: Creating a new Resource: Auto-Generated Schema

2.5 Connect Data Sources to GraphQL

The data that is exposed via the GraphQL API is pulled from data sources. Only connected data sources can be mapped to the API in the resolvers (see section 2.6 and chapter 5). In this section, we learn how to manage connected data sources (see section 2.5.1) and add new data sources (see section 2.5.2).

2.5.1 Data Sources

The data source can be managed on the data source screen shown in Figure 2.9. We can see a list of connected data sources for this API. On this screen, we can edit one of the data sources or add a new data source.

The scope of a data source connection is the API. Once a data source connection has been established, it is available for the complete API and can be used in all resolvers within the same API.

Figure 2.9: Overview of Connected Data Sources

2.5.2 Add a New Data Source

We can add a data source of any of the supported types, including Amazon DynamoDB tables, AWS Lambda functions, and the search capability of Amazon Elasticsearch.

Figure 2.10: Wizard for Creating a new Data Source

To add a new data source, we start on the data sources page on the AppSync API dashboard shown in Figure 2.10, and click on *New* to add a new data source. A wizard opens as depicted in Figure 2.10. Let's follow the wizard:

- Give the data source a friendly name, such as *"My first DynamoDB table"*.

- Choose the type of the data source, such as *Amazon Dy-namoDB table.*

- Choose the appropriate region, where the data is hosted.

- Choose a database table. Then either choose an existing role that has IAM permissions for PutItem and Scan for your table, or simply create a new IAM role.

The wizard gives us the possibility to generate GraphQL schema elements for the newly added data source, including types, queries and mutations, as shown in Figure 2.11.

Define an object type to hold data for this table.

```
1   # Object type that represents objects stored in the Amazon DynamoDB table named: AppSyncCommentTable-mi2wdJqr.
2 ▾ type AppSyncCommentTableMi2wdJqr {
3       # Key attributes. Changing these may result in unexpected behavior.
4       commentId: String!
5       eventId: String!
6
7       # Index attributes. Changing these may result in unexpected behavior.
8       createdAt: String
9
10      # Add additional non-key attributes below.
11
12  }
```

The following will be merged into your schema.

```
1 ▾ extend type Query {
2       getAppSyncCommentTableMi2wdJqr(eventId: String!, commentId: String!): AppSyncCommentTableMi2wdJqr
3       listAppSyncCommentTableMi2wdJqrs(first: Int, after: String): AppSyncCommentTableMi2wdJqrConnection
4       queryAppSyncCommentTableMi2wdJqrsByLSIAppSyncCommentTableByEventIdCreatedAt(eventId: String!, first: Int, after
5   }
6
7 ▾ extend type Mutation {
8       createAppSyncCommentTableMi2wdJqr(input: CreateAppSyncCommentTableMi2wdJqrInput!): AppSyncCommentTableMi2wdJqr
9       updateAppSyncCommentTableMi2wdJqr(input: UpdateAppSyncCommentTableMi2wdJqrInput!): AppSyncCommentTableMi2wdJqr
10      deleteAppSyncCommentTableMi2wdJqr(input: DeleteAppSyncCommentTableMi2wdJqrInput!): AppSyncCommentTableMi2wdJqr
11  }
```

Figure 2.11: Generating Schema Fragments based on a new Data Source

Realize that this is an option. We do not have to take the automatically generated GraphQL schema fragments. Sure it is convenient, but if we prefer our schema to look differently, we are not forced to rely on the generated 1:1 relationship between database table and GraphQL schema.

34

2.6 Resolver for Mapping

In GraphQL the mapping between GraphQL query and data source is done by a number of resolver functions. There is typically one resolver function per field. The resolver functions are managed on the schema page on the AppSync dashboard.

Figure 2.12: Management of Resolver Function on the Schema Page

On the right-hand side of the schema page (see Figure 2.12) we can attach a resolver function to each field of the schema. To attach a new resolver or to edit an existing resolver, follow these steps:

- Start on the schema page in AWS AppSync

- Click on the query type on the right.

- Click on "Attach/Edit resolver" button, so the "Edit resolver" page opens, as shown in Figure 2.13

- Choose the data source adapter created previously on the the "Edit resolver" page

- Define the request and response mappings on the "Edit resolver" page

Figure 2.13: Specify the AppSync Resolver

As you can observe in Figure 2.13, an AppSync Resolver consists of three parts, which will be described in the following sections:

1. Selection of a data source (see section 2.6.1 for details)

2. Specification of a request mapping (see section 2.6.2 for details)

3. Specification of a response mapping (see section 2.6.3 for details)

The specification of the request and response mappings for the resolver is a software engineering task that is massively supported by the AppSync tooling.

2.6.1 Data Source

A connected data source (see section 2.5) needs to be specified, that will be used in request and response mapping. Only connected data sources can be chosen. To connect a new data source, see sections 2.6 and 4.2.

2.6.2 Request Mapping

To map from GraphQL queries to the retrieval language of the data source, a request mapping is specified. The mapping is written using templates in the Velocity Templating Language (VTL). While it is possible to specify individual templates in VTL, we can choose from predefined templates, which are available for each operation of the supported data sources.

A template typically consists of a static and a dynamic part. The dynamic part depends on the parsed arguments from a GraphQL request, which are converted into elements of the data source request, e.g. a DynamoDB request. Learn more about request mappings in section 5.2.1.

2.6.3 Response Mapping

A response mapping specifies, how the result provided by the data source is mapped to a JSON representation of the respective GraphQL type. Example: `$utils.toJson($context.result)`. This example response mapping works as follows: AppSync makes the DynamoDB response available in the variable `$context.result`. In the response mapping, we simply transform this object structure into JSON, while leaving out all the metadata. Learn more about response mappings in section 5.2.1.

2.7 Test the API

Now, let's test the API. The AppSync API dashboard provides a test client that supports

- writing a query, mutation or response,

- sending it to the API endpoint and

- inspect the response.

Initially, our connected database is empty, so as a first operation, we need to send some information to it using a mutation.

```
mutation {
    createEvent(
            name:"API Days apidays.io"
            where:"Zurich"
            when:"September 2019"
            description:"Leading API Conference"
    ){
            id
            name
            where
            when
            description
    }
}
```

Notice, that we have only supplied the fields **name**, **where**, **when** and **description**, but the response includes the field **id**. The reason for this is, that the resolver is set up to automatically create an **id** for each new element.

Figure 2.14: Query Screen for API Testing

As one can observe in Figure 2.14, the operation is entered on the left-hand side of the query screen and the result appears on the right-hand side. Using the *Docs* button, we can reveal an additional column, showing the documentation of the API, as seen in Figure 2.15. We can then navigate in the documentation to the element we want to learn more about. Alternatively, we can just click on an element in our query/mutation and the documentation of this element opens up in the right-hand column.

Figure 2.15: Query Screen for API Testing with API Documentation

After we have added an event to the database with the mutation operation, we can list all the events with a query as follows.

```
query getAllEvents {
    listEvents{
        items{
            id
            name
            when
        }
    }
}
```

The functionality provided on the query page of the API dashboard is similar to the functionality provided by the GraphiQL tool (see section 10.5).

2.8 Build Client App

How can the API be integrated into an app? AppSync provides app templates for iOS, React Web, and React Native that can be used to call the AppSync API. The template is available on the AppSync dashboard (see Figure 2.16) and makes use of the

AppSync SDK. The AppSync SDK includes features for offline access, cache management, conflict resolution, and synchronization. It also provides convenient access to GraphQL APIs from the chosen client technology stack.

Figure 2.16: Example Dialog for Downloading the AppSync Client Code

To create a client, let's follow these steps:

- Chose the client technology stack. AppSync supports iOS, Android, React Web and React Native.

- We can use these templates by cloning the git repository for the respective client technology stack. For example, for the React Web template we use the following command to clone the repository.

```
git clone https://github.com/aws-samples/aws-mobile-appsync-events-starter-react
```

- Next, we install the dependencies using the npm command

```
npm install
```

- We download the individual AppSync config file from the provided download link and also the GraphQL schema, placing both of them into the src folder. We are now ready to run the client with the following command

```
npm start
```

- We should see our project running in the browser and we should now be able to add new events. Let's add a new event and check in our DynamoDB table if the new item was, in fact, added to our database.

3 GraphQL - Deep Dive

In this chapter, we dive deeper into GraphQL (see section 3.1), learn about the basic tools for interacting with GraphQL, such as the GraphQL schema definition language (see section 3.2) and the GraphQL query language (see section 3.3). If you are already familiar with GraphQL, you may skip this chapter.

3.1 More About GraphQL

In this section, we will study why there are two languages in GraphQL (see section 3.1.1), what the graph data structure in GraphQL is (see section 3.1.2), and how GraphQL relates to REST - the dominant philosophy for building APIs (see section 3.1.3).

3.1.1 Why are there Two Languages in GraphQL?

There are a query language and a schema definition language in GraphQL. These two languages have different purposes. The purpose of the schema definition language is to define the structure of the business data exposed by the GraphQL API. API providers use the schema definition language to specify the interface. The purpose of the query language is to interact with the GraphQL endpoint. Clients use the query language for reading data, writing data or subscribing to notifications. The schema serves as a constraint on the possible interactions.

The *GraphQL schema* can be compared to an à-la-carte menu in a restaurant, showing all the delicious dishes that clients may choose from. The menu has been defined by the owner of the restaurant, and it serves as an interface to the backend of the restaurant (a.k.a. kitchen). Ordering dishes that are not on the menu is not possible, simply because the kitchen is not prepared for it.

In this analogy, a *GraphQL query* is comparable to the order a client places in the restaurant. In this order, the client may select certain dishes from the menu, such as a starter and main dish. The same is true in GraphQL: in a GraphQL query, we refer to the elements that have been defined in the GraphQL schema.

3.1.2 What is the Graph in GraphQL?

A graph is a very generic data structure, so it should be possible to express the data of any application in the form of a graph. And this graph, formed by all application data, is what we call the graph in GraphQL.

With GraphQL we look at the overall set of data that is exposed by an API provider. All this data is exposed via a single endpoint. Compared to REST endpoints, the single GraphQL endpoint exposes a lot of data. This comprehensive set of data with its entities and relationships between the various entities forms the graph of GraphQL. To retrieve any data at all, one needs to navigate the graph.

When using other philosophies for building APIs, such as REST, we usually create several API endpoints and whatever is exposed by any single one of the API endpoints is typically not a generic graph, but rather a single entity or a list of entities. But there can be graph-like relationships across all API endpoints of an API provider. And this is, in fact, attempted by REST: resources are linked by URLs.

Both philosophies are capable of expressing application data in form of a graph, with GraphQL the graph is more explicit since it is served on a single endpoint.

3.1.3 What about REST?

Distributed systems, in general, are built with architectural styles of RPC, SOAP or REST, but when it comes to APIs, REST is the main paradigm. For a long time, REST was even thought to be the only accepted architectural style for building APIs.

GraphQL is neither the same as REST nor is GraphQL an extension of REST nor is GraphQL an improved version of REST. GraphQL provides a new philosophy for realizing APIs. That does not mean that GraphQL replaces REST and pushes it off the stage. There are good reasons to choose a RESTful API design.

GraphQL and REST are competing philosophies for building APIs. Each philosophy has its strength and its weaknesses. Looking at REST and GraphQL, there are a number of commonalities and major differences. When building a new API, it is a case-by-case decision to go with REST or GraphQL. If you are interested in a discussion on the differences, commonalities, strengths, and weaknesses of REST and GraphQL, check out the book *"REST & GraphQL - A Discussion on API Design"* [5].

3.2 GraphQL Schema Language

The GraphQL Schema Definition Language (SDL) or simply GraphQL schema language is a central piece of GraphQL, as it allows us to describe the structure or shape of the graph. The shape of the graph is expressed in the form of a schema. The schema defines a number of types, a number of relations between these types and methods or operations that can be performed on these types.

3.2.1 GraphQL Schema

Let's start with an example of a schema. The schema describes three types (`Book`, `Author`, and `Query`).

```
type Book {
   id: ID!
   title: String
   authors: [Author]
}
type Author {
        id: ID!
        name: String
}
type Query {
   books: [Book]
   book_by_id(id: ID!): Book
}
```

These types are related, i.e. there is s reference from `Query` to `Book` and from `Book` to `Author`. Another way of putting it is that they share an edge in the type graph. This type graph is visualized in figure 3.1.

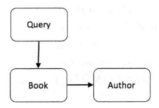

Figure 3.1: Example Type Graph

3.2.2 GraphQL Type System

GraphQL queries are strongly typed, based on a type system which is defined by the GraphQL schema (see section 3.2.1). The type system helps in various situations:

- During execution/resolution of a query, the type system helps to determine what to do next.

46

- When crafting queries, the introspection mechanism provided through the type system, allows us to do syntax-directed editing and guide us with respect to what is possible and available.

This type system consists of *predefined types* and *individual types*. Predefined types are built into GraphQL, such as the scalar types `Int`, `Float`, `Boolean` and `String` (see section 3.2.5). Individual types are defined by a GraphQL schema, using the GraphQL schema language, which we introduce in this chapter.

3.2.3 Types and Fields

A type is identified by its type name (`Book` or `Author` in our example in section 3.2.1) and consists of a number of fields. Our `Book` type consists of the fields `id`, `title`, and `authors`. Each of these fields has a type: The field `id` is of type `ID`, the field `title` is of type `String` and the field `authors` is of type array of `Author`.

3.2.3.1 Obligatory Fields - Nillable Fields

A field can be marked with an exclamation mark ! to indicate that the field is obligatory, e.g. the field `id` of type `ID` within the type `Book`.

```
type Book {
  id: ID!
  title: String
  authors: [Author]
}
```

If an obligatory field exists within a type, the type cannot be instantiated without providing a value for the obligatory field. In our example, the field `id` is obligatory for an instance of the type `Book`; thus the field `id` will not be null.

Fields that are not obligatory are called *nillable*. Fields in GraphQL are by default nillable, i.e. when fields are not marked with an exclamation mark. In the example above, the fields `title` and `authors` are nillable.

3.2.4 Root Types

With GraphQL queries we navigate in a graph. Where do we start navigating in a graph? In a graph, such as the one shown in Figure 3.1, the starting point determines where we can navigate and which nodes we can reach. Depending on where we start and depending on the structure of the graph, we may not be able to navigate all parts of the tree. This may be intentional or not.

In GraphQL we can define the starting points for navigating the tree, by defining fields in the so-called *root types*. A root type is a container for a certain type of operation. GraphQL offers three root types: `Query`, `Mutation`, and `Subscription`. Syntactically, they are just regular types with fields (see section 3.2.3). What is special about root types, is that they can be used as a starting point when formulating requests in the GraphQL query language (see chapter 3.3). Each GraphQL implementation must at least define a `Query` type and may define a `Mutation` and `Subscription` type.

```
type Query {
  books: [Book]
  book(title:String!): Book
  book_by_id(id:ID!): Book
}

type Mutation {
  addBook(title: String!): Book
}

type Subscription {
  bookAdded: Book
}
```

3.2.5 Scalar Types

Many *scalar types* are built-in to GraphQL, just as for any programming language. They comprise `Int`, `Float`, `Boolean` and

48

`String`. In addition, there is the built-in scalar type `ID`, which is used to uniquely identify an object.

```
scalar Isbn
type Book {
  id: ID!
  isbn: Isbn
  title: String
  authors: [Author]
}
```

Besides the built-in scalar types , it is possible to define and use custom scalar types , such as `Isbn` in the example above. Custom scalar types need to provide a serialization function and a parsing function. The execution semantics for such scalar types needs to be implemented in the resolver functions (see section 10.2).

3.2.6 Array

An *array* is used to express a list of objects of the same type. Arrays can be applied to scalar types and for object types, e.g `[int]` for a list of integers or `[Book]` for a list of `Books`. Arrays are used in GraphQL just as in any programming language.

3.2.7 Enum

An *enum* type has a limited set of values it can possibly take on. Defining the enum actually means defining this finite list of possible values. In the following example, the enum `TrafficLight` can take on any of the value `RED`, `GREEN` or `YELLOW`.

```
enum trafficLight{
  RED
  GREEN
  YELLOW
}
```

3.2.8 Interface

An *interface* is similar to a type definition, it defines a list of fields, but it is different since it cannot be instantiated. Types can implement an interface. Types that implement an interface are guaranteed to implement those fields of the interface.

```
interface Document{
  title: String
  text: String
  authors: [Author]
}
```

A regular type that implements the interface can extend the interface. In the following example, the type `Book` implements the interface `Document`.

```
type Book implements Document{
  id: ID!
}
```

The implementing type (`Book` in the example above) automatically contains the fields defined in the interface (`title`, `text`, and `authors` in the example above), they don't need to be mentioned explicitly. Additional fields can be defined in the type, such as the `id` field in the example above. To access the additional fields of a type implementing an interface in a query, we always need to make a distinction by type using inline fragments (see section 3.3.3.6).

3.2.9 Union

A *union* is a common type for several defining types. If an object is of a union type, it could be of any of its defining types. In the following, an object of type `Product` could be of type `Book` or of type `Software` or of type `Bread`.

```
union Product = Book|Software|Bread
```

So what is the difference between a union and an interface? The defining types of a union do not need to have any fields in common. With interfaces, however, the main purpose is to express common fields.

To access the fields of a union type in a query, we always need to make a distinction by type using the inline fragments (see section 3.3.3.6).

3.2.10 Input Types

Input types are used for passing input data in the form of arguments. Input types are used in mutations, when new objects are created or when objects are updated. When an instance of an input type is serialized, the data is formatted in JSON syntax.

The definition of input types looks exactly like the definition of regular object types, but with the keyword **input** instead of **type**. Note that input types cannot have fields of an object type, only scalar types, list types, and other input types. Despite the similar syntax, it is not possible to mix input types and regular types. To prevent mixing, it is a useful convention, to mark input types, e.g. by using the postfix **Input**.

```
input BookInput {
  title: String
  authors: [AuthorInput]
}
input AuthorInput {
      name: String
      books: [BookInput]
}
```

3.3 GraphQL Query Language

Clients use the GraphQL query language to interact with the GraphQL API.

How does this interaction work? The client first creates a GraphQL query using the GraphQL language and sends it to the API. The GraphQL API interprets the GraphQL query and responds with a JSON data structure.

What is a GraphQL query? A GraphQL query consists of one or more patterns (see section 3.3.1) and one method (see section 3.2.4). The patterns are matched against parts of the graph. The method determines how the matched parts of the graph are processed. The language provides methods for retrieving data, writing data and getting notified when the data changes. For example, with the query method, the matched parts of the graph are returned as results of the query.

3.3.1 Patterns

GraphQL queries consist of one or more patterns which are matched against the big graph containing all the data on the server. The patterns describe a subgraph of the big graph and are used to search for the relevant data in the big graph.

A pattern is expressed in terms of the relationships between objects and the fields the objects contain. This containment can be defined recursively. Let's have a look at an example of a pattern.

```
library {
  books {
    title
        id
  }
}
```

In the example, we see the pattern, which is used to search for a `library` object that contains `books` objects, which in turn contain both a `title` field and an `id` field. Curly brackets are used to express the containment. In front of the bracket is the name of the object (e.g. `library` or `books`), inside the brackets are the names of the fields of that object (e.g. `books` or `title` and `id`). Multi-level hierarchies can be built because a field can also be an object (e.g. `books`) which contains its own fields (e.g. `title` and `id`). When referring to several fields, they are each listed in a new line, without any separating commas or semicolons.

Speaking about semicolons: Note, that the GraphQL language is not JSON, even though it may look similar due to the use of curly brackets.

3.3.2 GraphQL Methods

Let's talk about the second ingredient of any GraphQL query besides the pattern: The GraphQL method. There are three methods in GraphQL:

- **query** is used for retrieval, for reading data (see section 3.3.3).

- **mutation** is used for modification, for writing data (see section 3.3.4).

- **subscription** is used for notification of changed data (see section 3.3.5).

In the following, we study each of the methods separately. These methods are represented by a type in the schema language.

3.3.3 GraphQL Query

To read data with GraphQL, the client uses the query method. In the pattern of this query, the client has to explicitly specify all the object and fields it is interested in. As a result of the query, the client gets exactly the objects and fields in the response that are specified in the request. Let's have a look at an example query.

```
query {
  books {
    title
  }
}
```

In this example, the client receives a list of books. Out of all the fields that book objects have, only the title will be returned for each book. Even though **books** might have other fields, these fields are not returned because they have not been explicitly requested in the query. Executing this query might result in the following data, which is returned in JSON format.

```
{
  "data": {
    "books": [
      {
        "title": "Book 1"
      },
      {
        "title": "Book 2"
      }
    ]
  }
}
```

What we first notice when using GraphQL for retrieval is that the structure of the response looks very similar to the query in the request. Query and response have the same shape. The query can be compared to a template in a template language. In the response, the client gets exactly the fields that are specified in the request, nothing additional, no surprises.

Just like functions in JavaScript, queries can be anonymous or named. For simplicity, we have so far worked with anonymous queries. The advantages of named queries are similar to those of named functions. If the function is given a name, it allows us to identify it easier later on, e.g. for debugging or logging. In the following example, we give the query the name myBookQuery.

```
query myBookQuery{
  books {
    title
  }
}
```

3.3.3.1 Objects

Inside the query method, one or more objects can be retrieved. But an object cannot be retrieved without explicitly specifying the fields that should be returned. The object and its fields need to be described in the corresponding GraphQL schema (see chapter 3.2).

```
query {
  books {
    title
  }
}
```

In the example above, the `books` object and its `title` field are retrieved.

3.3.3.2 Fields

Listing the fields of an object in GraphQL corresponds to a **SELECT** in SQL. Each object, such as `books`, has one or more fields. We can include the fields of an object into the result, by explicitly listing each one of the fields that we want to include. In this example, we include the `title` field.

```
query {
  books {
    title
  }
}
```

It is also possible to retrieve multiple fields. In the following example, we request the title and `id` fields.

```
query {
  books {
    title
        id
  }
}
```

In the previous example, both the `title` and `id` fields had a primitive type. GraphQL becomes really interesting when the field has an object type instead of a primitive type. Then the object field has further fields itself, as demonstrated in the following example.

```
query {
  books {
    title
        author {
          name
        }
  }
}
```

In the above example, the `books` object has a field **author** of type **Author**. And since the type **Author** has the field **name**, we can ask for this field in the query. When a field of object type is included in the query, a new level of nesting is created for this field. In the resulting data, the result tree gets deeper, i.e. gets a new level.

3.3.3.3 Arguments

Some objects or fields may accept arguments. An argument is used to put constraints on objects. Only objects which satisfy the constraints imposed by the argument are included in the result. An argument in GraphQL is comparable to a **WHERE** clause in SQL.

In the following example, out of all the books in the graph, only the **book** with **id 1234** shall be included in the result set.

```
query {
  book_by_id(id:"1234"){
    title
  }
}
```

Arguments are listed in round brackets right behind the field or object name. The arguments are named (**id** in our example). In most programming languages, functions identify the arguments by the order they are passed, but not in GraphQL. In GraphQL the arguments are identified and passed by their name (**id** in our example).

3.3.3.4 Alias

When selecting multiple fields in a query, we may also want to select the same field more than once. This would result in a naming conflict, as there would be two fields with the same name in the result. To avoid the naming conflict, we can rename a field with an alias. Here we introduce the alias **second_book**.

```
query {
  book_by_id(id:"1234"){
    title
  }
  second_book: book_by_id(id:"5678"){
    title
  }
}
```

3.3.3.5 Fragments

Some queries contain repeating elements. In this case, it is tedious to get consistent in the first place and tedious to maintain consistency. Let's have a look at an example with repeating elements.

```
query {
  book_by_id(id:"1234"){
    title
    author {
      name
    }
  }
  second_book: book_by_id(id:"5678"){
    title
    author {
      name
    }
  }
}
```

Repeating elements of a query can be factored out into so-called fragments. Fragments need to be defined once (using the **fragment** keyword) and can be applied multiple times (using the ... keyword). Rewriting the example with fragments results in the following.

```
query {
  book_by_id(id:"1234"){
    ...bookinfo
  }
  second_book: book_by_id(id:"5678"){
    ...bookinfo
  }
}

fragment bookinfo on Book{
  title
  author {
    name
  }
}
```

Note, that a fragment is defined for a specific type (see section 3.2.3), in our example, the fragment is specific for a **Book**.

3.3.3.6 Inline Fragments

Inline fragments are used to distinguish different types. It is similar to an **instanceof** operator in object-oriented programming languages. Inline fragments are for polymorphism, i.e. for `interface` (see 3.2.8) and `union` (see 3.2.9) types. It is not possible to statically determine all the fields available in an object, which implements the interface or union. This can only be accomplished at runtime with the use of the inline fragment. With inline fragments, we can check the type of an object at runtime and deal with the fields of that particular object.

Let's illustrate this concept with an example. We have the following type definitions in our schema (see chapter 3.2).

```
interface Document{
  title: String
  text: String
  authors: [Author]
}
type Book implements Document{
  id: ID!
}
type Article implements Document{
  magazine: String!
}
type Query{
  readingList: [Document]
}
```

The schema tells us that a `Document` can either be a `Book` or an `Article`. Both `Book` and `Article` contain the fields of `Document`, i.e. `title`, `text`, and `authors`, but each type has individual additional fields: a `Book` has an additional `id` field and an `Article` has an additional `magazine` field. A `Query` has a `readingList` of `Documents`.

How would a query for a `readingList` look like? Which fields would we be able to access?

```
query{
  readingList{
    title
    text
    authors{
      name
    }
  }
}
```

With the above query, we can only access the fields which are shared by all `Documents`, namely the fields `title`, `text`, and `authors`. We cannot access the specific fields of an `Article` or

Book in the **readingList**. This is because we would need to distinguish the actual type of a **Document**. For this purpose, we can use an inline fragment. In our example, we actually use two inline fragments, one for **Book** and one for **Article**.

```
query{
  readingList{
    title
    text
    authors{
      name
    }
    ... on Book {
      id
    }
    ... on Article {
      magazine
    }
  }
}
```

As we have seen in the example above, inline fragments can be used on interfaces (see section 3.2.8) to access additional fields of implementing types. In union types (see section 3.2.9), inline fragments are even more important. Since the member types of a union in general share no fields, inline fragments have to be used for accessing any field in a union.

3.3.3.7 Variables

Variables can be used to pass different values into a query. When this value needs to be changed, the query itself can stay as it is, since it only references the variable name. This allows for reusing and validating the query, despite different values being used. Often, variables are used for filtering, i.e. as GraphQL arguments (see section 3.3.3.3). Let's have a look at an example of a variable usage in a query

```
query getSpecificBook($bookID: String = "1234"){
  book_by_id(id: $bookID){
    title
  }
}
```

In the above example, we filter for a book with a particular id. The id is supplied in the variable **$bookID**. Variables are declared right after the `query` keyword and the name of the query. Variables have the scope of the complete query. Variables need to have a type (primitive or object type). Moreover, variables may have a default value. When no value is passed to the variable explicitly, it will have the value of the default value. In the above example, a default value is specified for the variable `$bookID` and its value is ``1234''.

3.3.3.8 Directives

Directives can be used to dynamically include or exclude a part of a query. Dynamically means depending on the value of a boolean variable (see section 3.3.3.7 on variables); this boolean variable has to be declared just like any other variable. Directives are modelled as annotations in a query and can be attached to a `field` or a `fragment`. There are two types of directives: one to include (`@include` keyword) a part of the query and one to exclude (`@skip` keyword) a part of the query.

```
query getBooks($flag: boolean){
  books{
    title
        id @include(if: $flag)
  }
}
```

The above example includes the id field only if the value of `$flag` is `true`.

```
query getBooks($flag: boolean){
  books{
    title
        id @skip(if: $flag)
  }
}
```

The above example is similar to the first one, but the logic is reversed. It skips the id field if `$flag` is `true`, meaning it includes the id field only if the value of `$flag` is `false`.

60

3.3.4 GraphQL Mutation

Just as the `query` method is used for reading data, the `mutation` method is used for modifying, adding or writing data on the server with GraphQL. Let's have a look at an example of a typical mutation.

```
mutation {
  addBook(title: "New Book"){
    id
    title
  }
}
```

The above mutation creates a book object with the title ``New Book'' and adds it to the graph. The values for the fields of the newly created object are passed as arguments. Arguments are named and are identified based on their name - not based on their position in the argument list, as it is typical for programming languages.

After adding the book, the mutation returns the newly created book object. However, it does not return the complete book object with all its attributes, but only the explicitly listed attributes of the new book: `id` and `title` in the example.

3.3.5 GraphQL Subscription

Modern clients need to get near real-time updates that get triggered when something changes on the server. For example, an instant messaging app needs to get notified, when a new message arrives on the server, or a weather app needs to get notified when a weather warning gets published.

REST does not provide any built-in support for such notifications from the server; thus notifications are often realized by polling or by webhooks. Learn more about webhooks and polling in this book [4].

- With polling, the client periodically sends requests to the server, to check if any new data is available. The client

61

usually needs to poll on an endpoint that returns a list of elements and compares the retrieved list against the previously retrieved list in order to find the new elements. Polling is expensive for both client and server, as it binds a lot of resources.

- With webhooks, the server calls the client, whenever new data becomes available. To set this up, the client first needs to register an endpoint that gets called by the server when a certain type of event happens. In order to receive events, the client needs to be able to expose an endpoint that can receive the events.

GraphQL offers subscriptions as a built-in mechanism for realizing notifications. After the client has subscribed to an event, it gets notified by the server when new events occur.

The first step of using GraphQL subscriptions is for the client to send a subscription request to the GraphQL API. The request specifies both the event (`bookAdded` in the example) to observe and the data (`id` and `title` of the newly added book), which should be sent from the server to the client, when the event is actually triggered.

```
subscription {
  bookAdded {
    id
    title
  }
}
```

What triggers a notification? In most cases, a notification is triggered by a modification of the data inside the graph, i.e. by a mutation. This means that an event handler needs to be installed inside the implementation of the mutation. In rare cases, a notification could be triggered by an external event, which is not directly accessible inside the graph or only accessible in aggregated form. An example is sensor data, of which a single measurement may be used as a trigger, whereas the graph only contains aggregated sensor data and no single measurements.

3.4 GraphQL API Design Methodology

3.4.1 API Design Approach

The fundamental idea is to design APIs as a digital product in its own right. Being a digital product, the API needs to be consumer-oriented. Now what does that mean and who are the consumers of an API?

3.4.2 Consumer-Oriented API Design

The consumers of an API are the various developers building clients with the API. And the essence of consumer-orientation is knowing the consumers including their needs and desires and putting these needs and desires of the API consumers first when designing the API. We need to know our prototypical API consumers, their needs, and the architecture of the solutions they are building. Our API should be as simple, clean, clear and approachable as possible from their perspective, i.e. from the perspective of the prototypical API consumers. It is important to stress this aspect since internal constraints and legacy systems otherwise tend to dominate API design.

3.4.2.1 Reusability

Consumer-oriented design can sometimes lead into the trap of basically designing an API for one customer only, i.e. designing for the very narrow needs of one consumer only. Instead, APIs need to be reusable products that can be reused by various consumers and in various use cases.

Despite being consumer-oriented, a product also needs to be somewhat generic, so it can be used by a wide range of customers. The API needs to be reusable in various solutions.

3.4.2.2 API Product Design

The basic process for GraphQL API design is no different than the basic process for API design of REST APIs [2]. If we design APIs as reusable products and design them from the perspective of the prototypical API consumers, then we are on the way to build consumer-oriented APIs – APIs that our consumers will love.

3.4.3 GraphQL API Design Phases

Let's start with an overview of the phases of this API design approach. Each phase of this approach consists of a creative part and a verification part. During the creative part an artifact is crafted, during the verification part early feedback on the artifact is collected. In each phase of the design and development journey, feedback from the consumers is elicited. It is important to collect the feedback as early as possible when changes to the API are still possible, are relatively simple and can be implemented with low risk, low effort, and low costs.

This design approach is meant to be used iteratively. There are small iterations which are triggered by the verification part of the same phase. And there are also big iterations, which are triggered by one of the later verification phases and require going back to the creative part of an earlier phase. Keep in mind, that in an iterative and agile approach, not all information and requirements about the constructed artifact need to be available in the beginning, but new and more detailed information and insights are gathered and integrated during each iteration. We need to get feedback from customers on the API design and build the GraphQL API outside-in. This means we need to start from the needs of the API consumer towards the existing legacy systems. And not the other way!

Our proposed API design approach is organized in six phases.

3.4.3.1 Phase 1: Domain Analysis

Domain analysis should get us thinking from an API consumer perspective: Who are the consumers of the API? What is the purpose of the API? Which API solutions do the consumers plan to build with the API? Which other API solutions would be possible with the API? How does an API consumer prefer to interact with the data delivered by the API?

3.4.3.2 Phase 2: Architectural Design

In the architectural design phase, we choose a server architecture, an API philosophy, and an architectural style for realizing the API. In the scope of this book, let's assume we choose a three-level server architecture with GraphQL as our API philosophy in the front-facing layer.

3.4.3.3 Phase 3: Prototyping

For prototyping a GraphQL API we need to define a schema (see chapter 3.2), which contains all the relevant types in the type graph. We use automatically created mock data, to simulate the response of the API and get some first feedback on the API design. In this phase, we can iterate multiple times by extending the schema and collecting feedback based on the mocked API.

3.4.3.4 Phase 4: Implementation

When implementing for production, we gradually move away from the use of mocked data, towards real data and real backend systems. At this point, the accidental complexity of the organically grown legacy systems may hit us and the API developers. In the implementation phase, non-functional properties come into focus, such as stability, performance, and security.

3.4.3.5 Phase 5: Publication

As soon as the GraphQL API is published, it needs to stay backward compatible with the originally published version. Only backward compatible changes are possible. Knowing about this hard cut imposed with initial publication of the GraphQL API, we need to ask if we have tested enough and have received enough consumer feedback to be confident to take the big leap of publishing the API.

3.4.3.6 Phase 6: Maintenance

During the maintenance phase, bugs and issues may be resolved, but also new functionality may be introduced, as long as it is backward compatible: functionality and fields may be added without breaking clients, but removing functionality or fields is not permitted.

Further down the line, we want to learn whether and why consumers use the API. We need to observe the metrics of our API to learn how consumers use the API. This cannot be based on analytics alone, but we need to communicate with our API consumers one-on-one and build an active community.

3.4.4 Number of APIs

How many GraphQL APIs should a company have? The power of GraphQL can only be fully utilized if all relevant data is within the same graph. As much data as possible should be linked to the same graph. This graph can then be exposed in one GraphQL API. It thus makes sense to have the complete API portfolio in one and the same GraphQL API.

3.4.5 Versioning

> Successful software always
> gets changed.
>
> ―――――――――――――――
> *Frederick P. Brooks*

Managing change and evolution in software systems is never easy, but it is especially difficult to manage change in loosely-coupled distributed systems, such as API solutions. Already a small change in the API is enough to break some of the clients consuming the API. From the perspective of the API consumer, longevity and stability are important aspects of published APIs. When APIs are published, they become available for consumers and it has to be assumed that the consumers build apps with the APIs. Published APIs cannot be changed in an agile manner. At least, APIs need to stay backward (and forward) compatible, so that old clients do not break and new clients can use the new and improved features.

3.4.5.1 Types of API Changes

People may want to change various aspects of published APIs. Are all of these changes equally severe for the clients? In this section, we analyze potential changes and classify them according to their severity. Severe changes are those changes that are incompatible (see section 3.4.5.1) and break a client. Not so severe are those API changes, that do not impact the client. They are called backward compatible (see section 3.4.5.1).

Backward Compatible Changes An API is backward compatible if an unchanged client can interact with a changed API. The unchanged client should be able to use all the functionality that was offered by the old API. If a change is supposed to be backward compatible, certain changes to the API are prohibited, while others are possible. The following is a list of backward compatible changes:

- Adding fields

- Adding types

- Adding queries, mutations, and subscriptions

Incompatible Changes   If a change to the API breaks the client, the change was incompatible. In general, removing and changing aspects of the API leads to incompatibilities. Here is a non-exhaustive list of incompatible changes:

- Removing existing fields

- Changing existing fields

- Removing types

- Removing queries, mutations or subscriptions

3.4.5.2 No Versioning in GraphQL APIs

Since evolution is difficult to manage, APIs should ideally be built in such a manner, that evolution becomes practically unnecessary and that any foreseeable changes can be realized as compatible changes. The versioning issue in GraphQL is not as severe as in other philosophies for building APIs. In GraphQL, the client needs to decide on the shape of the response when sending a request. A GraphQL API only returns the fields that are explicitly requested by the client.

Of course, the client can only choose from the available fields. GraphQL supports building backward compatible APIs. This means, that additional fields, additional types, additional queries, mutations, and subscriptions can be added. But existing fields cannot be changed or removed. No fields can be removed from existing types, and no types, queries, mutations or subscriptions can be removed.

An often-raised concern of avoiding versioning is that we have to deal with ever-growing API responses, as evolution allows for adding, but not for removing fields. With GraphQL the impact is much smaller: Only the size of the schema would grow and it might be harder to find the right field that is needed in the given situation. But the size of the actual response would not automatically grow when the schema grows since the response only contains the fields which are explicitly requested by the client.

4 AppSync Schema & Data Sources

When creating any GraphQL application (see section 1.2.4), the first step is always creating a schema definition – a definition of the data served by the API. We study the AppSync schema in section 4.1. The second step for a data-centric API is to define, where the API gets its data. And on a practical side, we connect our API implementation to data sources, such as databases, services, APIs or search domains. We study the types of data sources supported by AppSync in section 4.2 and also explain how they are used. AppSync provides additional support for the first two steps: In case we have an existing DynamoDB table, we would need to first create an appropriate schema and then connect the defined schema to a data source. AppSync allows us to automate these steps and offers a wizard for generating a new schema based on an existing database table. We study this feature in section 4.3.

4.1 AppSync Schema

There are two important questions regarding the AppSync schema. We answer the first question *"What is the AppSync Schema?"* in section 4.1.1 and the second question *"How to Get the AppSync Schema?"* in section 4.1.2.

4.1.1 What is the AppSync Schema

The AppSync schema is a GraphQL schema. To describe it we use the schema definition language introduced in section 3.2.

As depicted in Figure 4.1, the schema describes types, queries, mutations, and subscriptions. Types can be seen as the data structures exposed by the API. They are linked to other types. Queries are the *"getter"* functions, used for read-only access. Mutations are the *"setter"* functions, used for write access. Subscriptions are the real-time hooks, allowing apps to observe changes to the data in near-real-time.

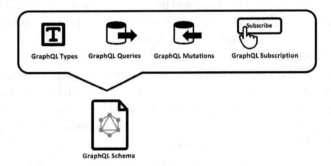

Figure 4.1: GraphQL Schema: Types, Queries, Mutations, and Subscriptions

4.1.2 How to Create an AppSync Schema

When creating any GraphQL application, the first step is always creating a schema definition – a definition of the data served by the API. There are several approaches for creating a GraphQL schema. It all depends on the starting point.

If the data that is to be exposed by the GraphQL API already exists in a database, which is reasonably structured, we can model the GraphQL schema after the existing database schema.

72

Some manual work will get the desired results. But in this situation, we might not have to create the schema manually. AppSync provides automated schema creation support that we can use, if we have the data in one of the databases technologies that are natively supported by AppSync. The schema creation support will mirror the existing database schema in a GraphQL schema.

In case we start on a green field and there are no databases that can be used as a starting point for the schema, the GraphQL schema needs to be specified manually. But once this is done, we can generate the database and tables automatically based a GraphQL schema definition. We can use the GraphQL schema editor provided by AppSync. It is quite user-friendly and comes with search and auto-complete capabilities. Go to the schema editor and add a new type in the GraphQL Schema. Click *Create Resources*. A new screen opens, as shown in Figure 4.2: Select the new type and give a name to the new table created in the backend database. New GraphQL operations are added to the schema and a new table in the data source is created.

Figure 4.2: Create Resources

So, once the type is defined in GraphQL, the getter, setter, and database table can be generated, instead of writing the respective code in the schema. The resulting generated schema is presented in Figure 4.3.

Figure 4.3: Create Resource - Generated Schema

4.2 AppSync Data Sources

Once the schema of the AppSync API is defined, we can connect
one or multiple data sources to the AppSync API. AppSync supports a number of AWS technologies as data sources (see Figure
4.4), such as an Amazon DynamoDB table, an AWS Lambda
function, or search capability of Amazon Elasticsearch. To be
able to access these data sources, we need to connect the data
sources.

In the following, we address for each data source technology
the following questions: (1) In which situation should we choose
this data source technology? (2) How do we create a data source
adapter to connect to the respective data source technology?

4.2.1 Amazon DynamoDB

Connect the DynamoDB data source like this:

Figure 4.4: AppSync Data Sources

- Go to the Data Sources page on the AppSync API dashboard, and choose *New*.

- Give the data source a friendly name, such as *"My DynamoDB data source"*.

- Choose *Amazon DynamoDB Table* as the type.

- Choose the appropriate AWS region, in which the DynamoDB is hosted.

- Choose the database table. Then either choose an existing role that has IAM permissions for the operations PutItem and Scan for the table, or create a new role with these permissions.

4.2.2 AWS Lambda

Via AWS Lambda functions it is possible to integrate a variety of data sources, such as third-party services and APIs and proprietary databases (which are e.g. hosted on EC2). It is even possible to aggregate and merge data from various sources. Typical data sources behind a lambda function are

- Existing REST services

- Existing SOAP services

- Existing GraphQL services

- AWS database technologies

- Other database technologies, not natively supported by AWS, which are deployed on an EC2 instance.

Connect the Lambda data source like this:

- Go to the Data Sources page on the AppSync API dashboard, and choose *New*.

- Give the data source a friendly name, such as *"My Lambda data source"*.

- Choose *AWS Lambda* as the type.

- Choose the appropriate AWS region, in which your Lambda function is hosted.

- Choose the Lambda function. Then either choose an existing role that has IAM permissions for invoking the Lambda function, or create a new role with the appropriate permissions.

4.2.3 Amazon Elasticsearch

Connect the data source like this:

- Go to the Data Sources page on the AppSync API dashboard, and choose *New*.

- Give the data source a friendly name, such as *"My Elasticsearch data source"*.

- Choose *Amazon Elasticsearch* as the type.

- Choose the appropriate AWS region, in which the Elasticsearch domain is hosted.

- Choose the Elasticsearch domain. Then either choose an existing role that has IAM permissions for searching the Elasticsearch domain, or create a new role with the appropriate permissions.

4.3 Automated Schema Creation

4.3.1 Schema Generation

AppSync offers a wizard for creating a new schema (and a new data source) based on an existing database table.

Figure 4.5: Creating a New Data Source

To add a new data source, let's go to the *Data Sources* page on the AppSync dashboard and click on *New* and follow the wizard.

This wizard page is displayed in Figure 4.5. It guides us through the following steps:

- Give the data source a friendly name, such as "My first data source".

- Choose the type of the data source, such as Amazon DynamoDB Table.

- Choose the appropriate region, where the data is hosted.

- Choose the existing database table. Then either choose an existing role that has IAM permissions for PutItem and Scan for the table, or create a new role.

In the end, the wizard provides the possibility to generate GraphQL schema parts (see Figure 4.6) for the newly added data source, including types, queries and mutations. The generated schema parts can be merged with the existing GraphQL schema.

AppSync supports creating a schema and resolvers from an existing table without having to write any code.

4.3.2 Generation of Schema and Database Table

AppSync offers the functionality to create a new database table based on an existing GraphQL type and it allows us to extend the GraphQL schema with queries and mutations for those GraphQL types. This functionality can be called from the schema page with the button *Create Resources*.

The *Create Resources* page opens. As input to the generation we simply select the GraphQL type and the name of a new table holding the type data, as shown in Figure 4.7. When confirming the resource creation, a new database table is generated.

In addition, the Getter and Setter can be generated in the form of a GraphQL Query and GraphQL Mutation, as shown in Figure 4.8. The generated artifacts are integrated into and merged with the GraphQL schema.

Define an object type to hold data for this table.

```
1    # Object type that represents objects stored in the Amazon DynamoDB table named: AppSyncCommentTable-mi2wdJqr.
2  ▾ type AppSyncCommentTableMi2wdJqr {
3        # Key attributes. Changing these may result in unexpected behavior.
4        commentId: String!
5        eventId: String!
6
7        # Index attributes. Changing these may result in unexpected behavior.
8        createdAt: String
9
10       # Add additional non-key attributes below.
11
12   }
```

The following will be merged into your schema.

```
1  ▾ extend type Query {
2        getAppSyncCommentTableMi2wdJqr(eventId: String!, commentId: String!): AppSyncCommentTableMi2wdJqr
3        listAppSyncCommentTableMi2wdJqrs(first: Int, after: String): AppSyncCommentTableMi2wdJqrConnection
4        queryAppSyncCommentTableMi2wdJqrsByLSIAppSyncCommentTableByEventIdCreatedAt(eventId: String!, first: Int, after
5    }
6
7  ▾ extend type Mutation {
8        createAppSyncCommentTableMi2wdJqr(input: CreateAppSyncCommentTableMi2wdJqrInput!): AppSyncCommentTableMi2wdJqr
9        updateAppSyncCommentTableMi2wdJqr(input: UpdateAppSyncCommentTableMi2wdJqrInput!): AppSyncCommentTableMi2wdJqr
10       deleteAppSyncCommentTableMi2wdJqr(input: DeleteAppSyncCommentTableMi2wdJqrInput!): AppSyncCommentTableMi2wdJqr
11   }
```

Figure 4.6: Generating Schema Parts based on existing Database

Figure 4.7: Create Resources

Figure 4.8: Create Resource Schema

5 AppSync Resolvers

After the schema has been defined and the data sources have been connected to AppSync, the remaining step is mapping the queries and mutation operations to actual read and write operations on one of the connected data sources. This connection between GraphQL and the data sources is defined in the AppSync resolver (see section 5.1). Resolvers as a concept are known in plain-vanilla GraphQL as well.

The AppSync resolver uses some new concepts (see section 5.2), namely the request and response mapping and some new tools for efficiently specifying the resolver (see section 6), such as the velocity templating language (VTL).

5.1 What is an AppSync Resolver?

The concept of a resolver originates from GraphQL and is also valid in the context of AppSync. In the following, we first study the GraphQL resolver in section 5.1.1 and then the specific additions of the AppSync resolver in section 5.1.2.

5.1.1 GraphQL Resolvers

In GraphQL the mapping between GraphQL query and data source is done by a so-called *resolver*. For most GraphQL runtimes, the resolver is implemented by a number of functions, one function for each type of the GraphQL schema. The resolver function of a complex types recursively calls the resolver functions for the direct member fields of the complex type. The

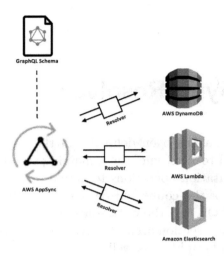

Figure 5.1: AppSync Resolvers

resulting call structure is a tree, ending in the "leaves" of primitive types that can be no more subdivided.

Let's recap: The resolver function is type-based; the function of complex types uses a recursive divide-and-conquer strategy; so what is the function of the primitive types? It gets the data from the data sources, for example, data from a database.

5.1.2 AppSync Resolvers

Resolvers in AppSync are based on the concept of GraphQL resolvers but are refined by additional concepts and supported by a set of new tooling.

5.1.2.1 Request and Response Mapping

AppSync introduces a new concept to the resolver function by splitting the resolver in two parts, each with distinctive responsibilities for mapping (see Figure 5.1). The *request mapping* maps

82

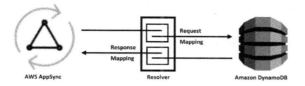

Figure 5.2: AppSync Resolver

data from the GraphQL query to the retrieval language of the data source and the *response mapping* maps data from the result delivered by the data source to a JSON object with the structure of the GraphQL schema and the specific types requested in the GraphQL request.

5.1.2.2 Template Language and Libraries

GraphQL is agnostic to the tooling and the choice of the right tool is up to the developer. In principle, resolvers can be written in any language, often they are written in JavaScript code.

A new concept in AppSync is the tooling support for expressing the request and response mappings in the resolver. AppSync provides tooling support and libraries for expressing request and response mappings. In AppSync, resolvers are written in a templating language called Velocity Templating Language (VTL), which is closer described in section 6.1. The Velocity Templating Language is integrated in AppSync, just as a library of predefined Velocity templates and a library of predefined mapping functions.

When writing several resolvers in VTL, it becomes obvious that creating templates is repetitive work: if written once, it is very simple to write the next one by a copy-and-paste operation. This is where predefined Velocity templates come in (see section 6.3).

5.2 AppSync Resolver Concepts

AppSync introduces a new concept to the resolver function by splitting the resolver in two parts, each with distinctive responsibilities for mapping.

- Part 1 is called *request mapping*. It maps data from the GraphQL query to the retrieval language of the data source.

- Part 2: is called *response mapping*: It maps data from the result delivered by the data source to the structure of the GraphQL schema and the specific types requested in the GraphQL query.

For most request mappings, the target language of the template is the language of the database, i.e. Amazon DynamoDB, the source language is GraphQL.

For most response mappings, templates simple pass data along, converting it to JSON `$utils.toJson($context.result)`.

5.2.1 Request Mapping

A request mapping describes how to translate a GraphQL request into instructions for a connected data source. In the request mapping, we need to convert the arguments defined in GraphQL to operations on the data source, e.g. to a Scan operation for DynamoDB. Since all DynamoDB operations follow a certain pattern, it is rather straightforward to capture the commonalities for certain database operations in predefined patterns. The following request mapping maps the after and first arguments of a GraphQL query to a Scan operation on a DynamoDB table.

```
{
    "version" : "2017-02-28",
    "operation" : "Scan",
    "nextToken" : "${context.arguments.after}",
    "limit" : ${context.arguments.first}
}
```

84

5.2.2 Response Mapping

A response mapping describes how to translate the response received from a data source into a GraphQL response. In the response mapping, we need to convert the database records to JSON data structures, that (1) satisfy the constraints of the GraphQL schema and (2) include the fields that were requested. AppSync provides a library of commonly used response mapping functions, such as $utils.toJson($context.result).

The following example of a response mapping uses the Velocity templating language. The basic idea is to write a template in the target language, here JSON. It is a template, containing both static parts that are copied 1:1 to the response and dynamic parts with placeholders that first need to be resolved. When executing the template, the contained placeholders are replaced by actual values.

```
$utils.toJson($context.result)
```

6 AppSync Resolver Tooling

AppSync takes a lot of weight from the shoulders of a GraphQL developer. What is left is the schema definition and specifying the resolver. And even for the remaining bit, for specifying the resolver, AppSync provides support through dedicated tools. AppSync natively supports the Velocity Templating Language VTL (see section 6.1). When using VTL, resolvers do not need to be programmed, they can be configured. And on top of that, AppSync even provides a library of predefined templates (see section 6.3) that can be used as a starting point for personalizing and configuring resolvers.

6.1 Velocity Templating Language

When implementing a GraphQL resolver from scratch, we would typically write the resolver implementation in a programming language, such as JavaScript. AppSync makes writing resolvers more efficient since it offers a library of resolver templates and provides a framework for specifying resolvers as mappings in the Velocity Templating Language VTL.

To be effective and efficient at specifying mappings in VTL, it makes sense to know VTL. In this section, we introduce the basics of VTL. It is, however, not a complete introduction to VTL, the intention of this section is merely to get started with the basic VTL needed for writing simple GraphQL resolvers. VTL is a powerful language with many advanced features. For advanced questions regarding VTL, consult the VTL user guide [10].

VTL is made for the purpose of expressing mappings or transformation in a declarative manner, without having to implement them on an operational level. The idea of VTL is to write a template with placeholders. The template is basically an example written in the target language. There are two types of placeholders: references and directives.

References are used for reading access, to access values from a variable, function or property. Learn more about references in section 6.1.1.

Directives are used for writing access, e.g. to set values and to adjust the structure of the template. Don't mix up directives in GraphQL (see section 3.3.3.8) with directives in VTL; they have nothing in common except for their name. Learn more about VTL directives in section 6.1.2.

6.1.1 References

References are used to access data and can be placed anywhere in the VTL template. Syntactically, references are identified by a leading $ in the name. The data that can be accessed via references is held in a variable, held in a property or it can be calculated by a method. To access the value of a variable, simply place the reference in the template.

```
Hello $name
```

To access the data of a property, simply place the reference in the template.

```
Your address is $customer.Address
```

And to access the data calculated by a method, simply place the reference in the template.

```
Your address is $customer.getAddress()
```

References can be used anywhere within the template to output the value associated with the reference. References can also be used within directives for logical operations or control structures (see section 6.1.2).

6.1.2 Directives

Directives are used to write values to variables or properties and to adjust the structure of the template. Directives can access variables, properties or methods dynamically and assign values. Syntactically, directives are marked with **#**.

```
#set( $monkey = "banana" )
```

The above statement creates a variable **$monkey** and assigns the value ``banana'' to it. If the variable **$monkey** already exists, its value will be overwritten by the **#set** directive. If the variable **$monkey** does not exist, it will be created before assigning its initial value.

```
#set( $monkey = $bill )
```

The above statement creates a variable **$monkey** and assigns the value of the variable **$bill** to it.

6.1.3 Conditional Directive

The condition is a directive to make binary either-or decisions. References are used in the comparison part.

```
#if($foo == $bar)it's true!#{else}it's not!#end
```

6.1.4 Foreach Directive

The foreach directive is used to loop through all elements in a list and perform the same operation for each element.

```
#foreach( $customer in $customerList )
<tr>
<td>$foreach.count</td>
<td>$customer.Name</td>
</tr> #end
```

The example above creates an HTML table containing two columns with a unique number and the name of the customer.

6.1.5 Include

The include directive is used to place a verbatim copy of the content of the file into the output.

```
#include("disclaimer.txt")
```

6.1.6 Parse

Parse is used to include another file and interpret the content of the file as a Velocity Template, containing directives and references.

```
#parse("dynamic_content.vtl")
```

6.1.7 Comments

Whatever is placed in between comment delimiters is ignored and not resolved as output of the template. There are both one-line comments and multi-line comments.

```
## This is a one-line comment.**

#**
This is a multi-line comment.
This is the second line.
*#
```

6.2 AppSync Variables and Functions

AppSync defines a number of variables and functions that can be used inside the Velocity templates realizing resolvers, whether these templates are custom-defined or predefined AppSync templates. How do AppSync variables get their values? The values of AppSync variables are populated by the AppSync framework itself and can be used within a Velocity template.

90

6.2.1 Context Variable

The context variable allows us to access data that was collected or produced outside the Velocity template. The context object contains information about resolver invocation, about the GraphQL request or the data source response, depending on when and where it is accessed. Here a list of fields of the context object:

arguments The GraphQL arguments made available in the Velocity resolver template.

source The results of the parent resolver.

result The results of this resolver, available in the response mapping.

identity The identity of the authenticated caller. The selection of available fields depends on the authentication method used (see also chapter 8):

- If API-Keys are used as the authentication method, no identity information is available
- If Amazon IAM is used as the authentication method, the following identity attributes are populated in the context object
    - accountId: AWS account ID of the caller
    - cognitoIdentityPoolId: identity pool ID associated with the caller
    - cognitoIdentityId: identity ID
    - sourceIp: IP address of the caller, and of intermediary gateway (x-forwarded-for HTTP header)
    - username: AWS user principal
    - userArn: IAM ARN

- If Amazon Cognito User Pools are used as the authentication method, the available identity information is based on the attributes provided in the OpenID Connect tokens

  - sub: uuid of the user

  - issuer: token issuer

  - username:

  - claims: object of attribute claims

  - sourceIp: IP address of the caller, and of intermediary gateway (x-forwarded-for HTTP header)

  - defaultAuthStrategy: DENY or ALLOW

Example for Using the Context Object

Let's imagine we have the following GraphQL query:

```
query {
    getPost(id: 1234) {
        postId
        title
        content
        author {
            id
            name
        }
    }
}
```

In the request mapping, we can expect a context object containing at least the following data:

```
{
    "arguments" : {
        "id" : "1234"
    },
    "identity" : {
        "sourceIp" : ["192.168.1.1"],
        "userArn" : "arn:aws:iam::4711:user/appsync",
        "accountId" : "4711",
        "user" : "steve_smith"
    }
}
```

We could use the context object `$context.arguments.id` inside a request mapping e.g. in the following manner to look up a `Post` by its `id` field in a DynamoDB table:

```
{
        "version" : "2017-02-28",
        "operation" : "GetItem",
        "key" : {
                "id" : { "S" : "${context.arguments.id}" },
        },
        "consistentRead" : true
}
```

In the response mapping, we can expect a context object containing e.g. the following data:

```
{
    "arguments" : {},
    "source" : {
        "createdAt" : "2018-05-28T17:47:47Z",
        "title" : "Brazil",
        "content" : "I want to tell you about my recent trip to Brazil ...",
        "postId" : "1234",
        "authorId" : "34521"
    },
    "result" : {
        "name" : "Steve",
        "joinDate" : "2018-01-01T17:47:47Z",
        "id" : "123"
    },
    "identity" : {
        "sourceIp" : ["192.168.1.1"],
        "userArn" : "arn:aws:iam::4711:user/appsync",
        "accountId" : "4711",
        "user" : "steve_smith"
    }
}
```

6.2.2 Generic Helper Functions

AppSync provides several utility functions that make it easier to work with the data in a resolver. This includes functions to convert between different encodings and formats, type checks, error handling, exception handling, checks for null values, and search with regular expressions.

$util.escapeJavaScript(String):String Escapes a string according to JavaScript rules

$util.urlEncode(String):String Encodes a string according to application/x-www-form-urlencoded

$util.urlDecode(String):String Decodes an application/x-www-form-urlencoded string

$util.base64Encode(byte[]):String Encodes a string according to base64

$util.base64Decode(String):byte[] Encodes a base64 encoded string

$util.parseJson(String):Object Creates a JavaScript object from a JSON string

$util.toJson(Object):String Serializes an object into a JSON string

$util.autoId():String Creates a UUID (128 bit)

$util.unauthorized() Throws an unauthorized error

$util.error(String) Throws a custom error

$util.error(String,String) Throws a custom error, allows specifying an errorType

$util.error(String,String,Object) Throws a custom error, allows specifying an errorType and a data field

$util.error(String,String,Object,Object) Throws a custom error, allows specifying an errorType, a data field, and an errorInfo

$util.appendError(String) Appends a custom error and will not interrupt the template evaluation, so that data can be returned to the caller.

$util.appendError(String,String) Appends a custom error, allows specifying an errorType

$util.appendError(String,String,Object) Appends a custom error, allows specifying an errorType and a data field

$util.appendError(String,String,Object,Object) Appends a custom error, allows specifying an errorType, a data field, and an errorInfo

$util.validate(boolean,String):void If the first argument evaluates to false, the method throws a CustomTemplateException with the message specified in the second argument

$util.validate(boolean,String,String):void If the first argument evaluates to false, the method throws a CustomTemplate-Exception with the message specified in the second argument and the error type specified in the third parameter

$util.validate(boolean,String,String,Object):void If the first argument evaluates to false, the method throws a CustomTemplateException with the message specified in the second argument, the error type specified in the third parameter and the data object specified in the last parameter.

$util.isNull(Object):boolean Returns true if the object is null

$util.isNullOrEmpty(String):boolean Returns true if the string is null or an empty string

$util.isNullOrBlank(String):boolean Returns true if the string is null or a blank

$util.defaultIfNull(Object,Object):Object Returns first argument if it is not null, otherwise, returns second argument

$util.defaultIfNullOrEmpty(String,String):String Returns the first string if it is not null or empty, otherwise, returns the second string

$util.defaultIfNullOrBlank(String,String):String Returns the first string if it is not null or blank, otherwise, returns the second string

$util.isString(Object):boolean Returns true if the object is a string

$util.isNumber(Object):boolean Returns true if the object is a number

$util.isBoolean(Object):boolean Returns true if the object is a boolean

$util.isList(Object):boolean Returns true if the object is a list

$util.isMap(Object):boolean Returns true if the object is a map.

$util.typeOf(Object):String Returns a string describing the type of the argument, i.e. "Null", "Number", "String", "Map", "List", "Boolean", "Object".

$util.matches(String,String):boolean Returns true if the pattern in the first argument matches the second argument, using regular expression

6.2.3 Date and Time Helper Functions

The date and time helper functions allow us to generate timestamps, convert between various date and time formats, and parse date and time strings.

$util.time.nowISO8601():String Returns a String representation of UTC in ISO8601 format.

$util.time.nowEpochSeconds():long Returns the number of seconds from the epoch of 1970-01-01T00:00:00Z to now.

$util.time.nowEpochMilliSeconds():long Returns the number of milliseconds from the epoch of 1970-01-01T00:00:00Z to now.

$util.time.nowFormatted(String):String Returns a string of the current timestamp in UTC using the specified format from a String input type.

$util.time.nowFormatted(String,String):String Returns a string of the current timestamp for a timezone using the specified format and timezone from String input types.

$util.time.parseFormattedToEpochMilliSeconds(String,String):long Parses a timestamp passed as a String, along with a format, and return the timestamp as milliseconds since epoch.

$util.time.parseFormattedToEpochMilliSeconds(String,String,String):long Parses a timestamp passed as a String, along with a format and time zone, and return the timestamp as milliseconds since epoch.

$util.time.parseISO8601ToEpochMilliSeconds(String):long Parses an ISO8601 timestamp, passed as a String, and return the timestamp as milliseconds since epoch.

$util.time.epochMilliSecondsToSeconds(long):long Converts an epoch milliseconds timestamp to an epoch seconds timestamp.

$util.time.epochMilliSecondsToISO8601(long):String Converts an epoch milliseconds timestamp to an ISO8601 timestamp.

$util.time.epochMilliSecondsToFormatted(long,String):String
Converts an epoch milliseconds timestamp, passed as long, to a timestamp formatted according to the given format in UTC.

$util.time.epochMilliSecondsToFormatted(long,Str,Str):Str Conv an epoch milliseconds timestamp, passed as a long, to a timestamp formatted according to the given format in the given timezone.

6.2.4 List Helper Functions

The list helpers are functions that provide common operations for list data structures, such as removing items from a map or retaining items on a map for filtering use cases.

$util.list.copyAndRetainAll(List,List):List Makes a shallow copy of the list in the first argument, retaining only the items specified in the second argument.

$util.list.copyAndRemoveAll(List,List):List Makes a shallow copy of the list in the first argument, and removes all the items specified in the second argument.

6.2.5 Map Helper Functions

The map helpers are functions that provide common operations for map data structures, such as removing items from a map or retaining items on a map for filtering use cases.

$util.map.copyAndRetainAllKeys(Map,Map):Map Makes a shallow copy of the map in the first argument, retaining only the items specified in the second argument.

$util.map.copyAndRemoveAllKeys(Map,Map):Map Makes a shallow copy of the list in the first argument, and removes all the items specified in the second argument.

6.2.6 DynamoDB Helper Functions

$util.dynamodb contains helper methods that make it easier to write and read data to Amazon DynamoDB. Make mapping primitive types and Lists to the proper DynamoDB input format automatically.

$util.dynamodb.toDynamoDB(Object):Map General object conversion tool for DynamoDB that converts input objects to the appropriate DynamoDB representation.

$util.dynamodb.toDynamoDBJson(Object):String The same as $util.dynamodb.toDynamoDB(Object):Map, but returns the DynamoDB attribute value as a JSON encoded string.

$util.dynamodb.toString(String):String Convert an input string to the DynamoDB string format. This returns an object that describes the DynamoDB attribute value.

$util.dynamodb.toStringJson(String):Map Comparable to the function $util.dynamodb.toString(String):String, but returns the DynamoDB attribute value as a JSON encoded string.

$util.dynamodb.toStringSet(List<String>):Map Converts list with Strings to the DynamoDB string set format. This returns an object that describes the DynamoDB attribute value.

$util.dynamodb.toStringSetJson(List<String>):String Same as $util.dynamodb.toStringSet(List<String>):Map, but returns the DynamoDB attribute value as a JSON encoded string.

$util.dynamodb.toNumber(Number):Map Converts a number to the DynamoDB number format. This returns an object that describes the DynamoDB attribute value.

$util.dynamodb.toNumberJson(Number):String The same as
$util.dynamodb.toNumber(Number):Map, but returns the
DynamoDB attribute value as a JSON encoded string.

$util.dynamodb.toNumberSet(List<Number>):Map Converts
a list of numbers to the DynamoDB number set format.
This returns an object that describes the DynamoDB attribute value.

$util.dynamodb.toNumberSetJson(List<Number>):String The
same as $util.dynamodb.toNumberSet(List<Number>):Map,
but returns the DynamoDB attribute value as a JSON encoded string.

$util.dynamodb.toBinary(String):Map Converts binary data en-
coded as a base64 string to DynamoDB binary format.
This returns an object that describes the DynamoDB attribute value.

$util.dynamodb.toBinaryJson(String):String Comparable to the
function $util.dynamodb.toBinary(String):Map, but returns
the DynamoDB attribute value as a JSON encoded string.

$util.dynamodb.toBinarySet(List<String>):Map Converts list
of binary data encoded as base64 strings to DynamoDB binary set format. This returns an object that describes the
DynamoDB attribute value.

$util.dynamodb.toBinarySetJson(List<String>):String Same
as $util.dynamodb.toBinarySet(List<String>):Map, but re-
turns the DynamoDB attribute value as a JSON encoded
string.

$util.dynamodb.toBoolean(boolean):Map Converts a boolean
to the appropriate DynamoDB boolean format. This returns an object that describes the DynamoDB attribute
value.

$util.dynamodb.toBooleanJson(boolean):String The same as $util.dynamodb.toBoolean(boolean):Map, but returns the DynamoDB attribute value as a JSON encoded string.

$util.dynamodb.toNull():Map Returns a null in DynamoDB null format. This returns an object that describes the DynamoDB attribute value.

$util.dynamodb.toNullJson():String Comparable to the function $util.dynamodb.toNull():Map, but returns the DynamoDB attribute value as a JSON encoded string.

$util.dynamodb.toList(List):Map Converts a list of object to DynamoDB list format.

$util.dynamodb.toListJson(List):String Comparable to the function $util.dynamodb.toList(List):Map, but returns the DynamoDB attribute value as a JSON encoded string.

$util.dynamodb.toMap(Map):Map Converts a map to DynamoDB map format.

$util.dynamodb.toMapJson(Map):String Comparable to the function $util.dynamodb.toMap(Map):Map, but returns the DynamoDB attribute value as a JSON encoded string.

$util.dynamodb.toMapValues(Map):Map Creates a copy of the map where each value has been converted to its appropriate DynamoDB format.

$util.dynamodb.toMapValuesJson(Map):String The same as $util.dynamodb.toMapValues(Map):Map, but returns the DynamoDB attribute value as a JSON encoded string.

$util.dynamodb.toS3Object(String,String,String):Map Converts the key (first argument), bucket (second argument) and region (third argument) into the DynamoDB S3 Object representation. This returns an object that describes the DynamoDB attribute value.

$util.dynamodb.toS3ObjectJson(String,String,String):String
The same as $util.dynamodb.toS3Object(String key, String bucket, String region):Map, but returns the DynamoDB attribute value as a JSON encoded string.

$util.dynamodb.toS3Object(String,String,String,String):Map
Converts the key (first argument), bucket (second argument) and region (third argument) and optional version (fourth argument) into the DynamoDB S3 Object representation. This returns an object that describes the DynamoDB attribute value.

$util.dynamodb.toS3ObjectJson(Str,Str,Str,Str):Str The same as $util.dynamodb.toS3Object(String key, String bucket, String region, String version):Map, but returns the DynamoDB attribute value as a JSON encoded string.

$util.dynamodb.fromS3ObjectJson(String):Map Accepts string value of a DynamoDB S3 Object and returns a map that contains the key, bucket, region and optional version.

6.3 AppSync Velocity Templates

In AppSync, we use Velocity templates for request and response mappings. Most predefined Velocity templates, however, are used for request mapping. For request mapping, the source language is GraphQL, the target language is the language of the database, i.e. Amazon DynamoDB. For response mapping, the source language is the language of the database, the target language is JSON, used according to the GraphQL type structure.

6.3.1 DynamoDB Resolver Templates

The AWS AppSyncDynamoDB resolver enables us to use GraphQL to store and retrieve data in existing Amazon DynamoDB tables in our account. This resolver works by enabling us to map an incoming GraphQL request into a DynamoDB request, and then map the DynamoDB response back to GraphQL/JSON. This section describes the predefined mapping templates for DynamoDB operations.

6.3.1.1 GetItem

Reading access to DynamoDB uses the GetItem request, which looks as follows:

```
{
        "version" : "2017-02-28",
        "operation" : "GetItem",
        "key" : {
                "foo" : ... typed value,
                "bar" : ... typed value
        },
        "consistentRead" : true
}
```

The fields of a GetItem request are defined by DynamoDB as follows:

version The DynamoDB version. As a value, only 2017-02-28 is supported. Required.

operation The DynamoDB operation. For a GetItem operation set the value to GetItem. Required.

key The key of the item in DynamoDB. Required.

consistentRead Advises DynamoDB to perform a strongly consistent read. Optional, default: false.

GetItem Request Mapping Template The template uses the arguments of the GraphQL query as keys for the DynamoDB

103

GetItem request. The AppSync framework makes the GraphQL query arguments available in the context object. It does this automatically without us having to configure anything. It retrieves these arguments via the context object as Velocity variables.

Let's imagine we have a GraphQL Query with the following signature

```
query getThing(foo: String!, bar: String!){ ... }
```

Then a request mapping in Velocity could be:

```
{
        "version" : "2017-02-28",
        "operation" : "GetItem",
        "key" : {
                "foo" : { "S" : "${context.arguments.foo}" },
                "bar" : { "S" : "${context.arguments.bar}" }
        },
        "consistentRead" : true
}
```

GetItem Response Mapping Template   The item returned from DynamoDB is converted into a GraphQL response in JSON. In addition, it is available in the context (`$context.result`). Thus, the response mapping template is a simple passthrough of data, realized by the following predefined mapping function:

```
$utils.toJson($context.result)
```

6.3.1.2 PutItem

Writing access to DynamoDB for new or existing entries uses the `PutItem` request. It may be used to create new entries or update existing ones. The overwrite behavior can be specified. The `PutItem` request looks as follows:

```
{
        "version" : "2017-02-28",
        "operation" : "PutItem",
        "key": {
                "foo" : ... typed value,
                "bar" : ... typed value
        },
        "attributeValues" : {
```

104

```
                "baz" : ... typed value
        },
        "condition" : {
                ...
        }
}
```

The fields of a `PutItem` request are defined by DynamoDB as follows:

version The DynamoDB version. As a value, only 2017-02-28 is supported. Required.

operation The DynamoDB operation. For a PutItem operation set the value to `PutItem`. Required.

key The key of the item in DynamoDB. Required.

attributeValues The attributes of the item to be put into DynamoDB. Optional.

condition The condition states the overwrite behavior if an entry with the given key already exists. Optional, default semantics: overwrite.

   expression The condition expression, which may contain variables. Required.

   expressionNames The substitutions for names, as a list of key-value pairs. The key is the name of a variable used in the expression, the value is an attribute name of the item in DynamoDB. Optional.

   expressionValues The substitutions for values, as a list of key-value pairs. The key is the name of a variable used in the expression, the value is a literal. Optional.

PutItem Request Mapping Template The template uses the arguments of the GraphQL mutation as keys for the DynamoDB PutItem request. The AppSync framework makes the GraphQL mutation arguments available in the context object. It does this automatically without us having to configure anything. It retrieves these arguments via the context object as Velocity variables.

Following is a mapping template for a GraphQL mutation.

```
mutation updateThing(foo: String!, bar: String!, name: String!, version: Int!)
```

If no item with the specified key exists, it will be created. If an item already exists with the specified key, it will be overwritten.

```
{
        "version" : "2017-02-28",
        "operation" : "PutItem",
        "key": {
                "foo" : { "S" : "${context.arguments.foo}" },
                "bar" : { "S" : "${context.arguments.bar}" }
        },
        "attributeValues" : {
                "name" : { "S" : "${context.arguments.name}" },
                "version" : { "N" : ${context.arguments.version} }
        }
}
```

PutItem Request Mapping Template with Condition Following is a mapping template for a GraphQL mutation

```
mutation updateThing(foo: String!, bar: String!, name: String!, expectedVersion: Int!)
```

This example checks to be sure the item currently in DynamoDB has the version field set to expectedVersion.

```
{
        "version" : "2017-02-28",
        "operation" : "PutItem",
        "key": {
                "foo" : { "S" : "${context.arguments.foo}" },
                "bar" : { "S" : "${context.arguments.bar}" }
        },
        "attributeValues" : {
                "name" : { "S" : "${context.arguments.name}" },
                #set( $newVersion = $context.arguments.expectedVersion + 1 )
                "version" : { "N" : ${newVersion} }
        },
        "condition" : {
                "expression" : "version = :expectedVersion",
                "expressionValues" : {
                        ":expectedVersion":
                                {"N":${context.arguments.expectedVersion}}}
        }
}
```

PutItem Response Mapping Template The item returned from DynamoDB is converted into a GraphQL response in JSON. In addition, it is available in the context (`$context.result`). Thus, the response mapping template is a simple passthrough of data, realized by the following predefined mapping function:

```
$utils.toJson($context.result)
```

6.3.1.3 UpdateItem

Writing access to DynamoDB for updating an existing entry uses the `UpdateItem` request. It may only be used to update existing entries. The `UpdateItem` request for DynamoDB looks as follows:

```
{
        "version" : "2017-02-28",
        "operation" : "UpdateItem",
        "key": {
                "foo" : ... typed value,
                "bar" : ... typed value
        },
        "update" : {
                "expression" : "someExpression"
                "expressionNames" : {
                        "#foo" : "foo"
                },
                "expressionValues" : {
                        ":bar" : ... typed value
                }
        },
        "condition" : {
                ...
        }
}
```

The fields of a `UpdateItem` request are defined by DynamoDB as follows:

version The DynamoDB version. As a value, only 2017-02-28 is supported. Required.

operation The DynamoDB operation. For a UpdateItem operation set the value to `UpdateItem`. Required.

key The key of the item in DynamoDB. Required.

update The update section describes how to update the item in DynamoDB.

> **expression** The update expression, which may contain variables. Required.

> **expressionNames** The substitutions for names, as a list of key-value pairs. The key is the name of a variable used in the expression, the value is an attribute name of the item in DynamoDB. Optional.

> **expressionValues** The substitutions for values, as a list of key-value pairs. The key is the name of a variable used in the expression, the value is a literal. Optional.

condition The condition states the overwrite behavior if an entry with the given key already exists. Optional, default: overwrite.

UpdateItem Request Mapping Template The template uses the arguments of the GraphQL mutation as keys for the DynamoDB UpdateItem request. The AppSync framework makes the GraphQL mutation arguments available in the context object. It does this automatically without us having to configure anything. It retrieves these arguments via the context object as Velocity variables.

Following is a mapping template for the GraphQL mutation

```
mutation upvote(id: ID!)
```

In this example, an item in DynamoDB has its upvotes and version fields incremented by 1.

```
{
        "version" : "2017-02-28",
        "operation" : "UpdateItem",
        "key" : {
                "id" : { "S" : "${context.arguments.id}" }
        },
        "update" : {
                "expression" : "ADD #votefield :plusOne, version :plusOne",
                "expressionNames" : {
```

```
            "#votefield" : "upvotes"
        },
        "expressionValues" : {
            ":plusOne" : { "N" : 1 }
        }
    }
}
```

UpdateItem Response Mapping Template   The item returned
from DynamoDB is converted into a GraphQL response in JSON.
In addition, it is available in the context ($context.result).
Thus, the response mapping template is a simple passthrough
of data, realized by the following predefined mapping function:

```
$utils.toJson($context.result)
```

6.3.1.4 DeleteItem

Writing access to DynamoDB for deleting an existing entry uses
the DeleteItem request. It may only be used to delete existing entries. The DeleteItem request for DynamoDB looks as
follows:

```
{
    "version" : "2017-02-28",
    "operation" : "DeleteItem",
    "key": {
        "foo" : ... typed value,
        "bar" : ... typed value
    },
    "condition" : {
        ...
    }
}
```

The fields of a DeleteItem request are defined by DynamoDB
as follows:

version The DynamoDB version. As a value, only 2017-02-28
is supported. Required.

operation The DynamoDB operation. For a DeleteItem operation set the value to UpdateItem. Required.

key The key of the item in DynamoDB. Required.

condition The condition states additional constraints/conditions that must be met for executing this operation. Optional, default semantics: overwrite.

> **expression** The condition, which may contain variables. Required.
>
> **expressionNames** The substitutions for names, as a list of key-value pairs. The key is the name of a variable used in the expression, the value is an attribute name of the item in DynamoDB. Optional.
>
> **expressionValues** The substitutions for values, as a list of key-value pairs. The key is the name of a variable used in the expression, the value is a literal. Optional.

DeleteItem Request Mapping Template The template uses the arguments of the GraphQL mutation operation as keys for the DynamoDB DeleteItem request. The AppSync framework makes the GraphQL mutation arguments available in the context object. It does this automatically without us having to configure anything. It retrieves these arguments via the context object as Velocity variables.

Following is a mapping template for the GraphQL mutation.

```
mutation deleteItem(id: ID!)
```

The argument `id` of type ID is required. If an item exists with this id, it will be deleted.

```
{
        "version" : "2017-02-28",
        "operation" : "DeleteItem",
        "key" : {
                "id" : { "S" : "${context.arguments.id}" }
        }
}
```

DeleteItem Request Mapping Template with Condition Following is a mapping template for a GraphQL mutation

```
mutation deleteItem(id: ID!, expectedVersion: Int!)
```

If an item exists with this id, it will be deleted, but only if its version field corresponds to the expectedVersion:

```
{
        "version" : "2017-02-28",
        "operation" : "DeleteItem",
        "key" : {
                "id" : { "S" : "${context.arguments.id}" }
        },
        "condition" : {
                "expression" :
                "attribute_not_exists(id) OR version = :expectedVersion",
                "expressionValues" : {
                        ":expectedVersion" :
                        { "N" : ${context.arguments.expectedVersion} }
                }
        }
}
```

DeleteItem Response Mapping Template The item returned from DynamoDB is converted into a GraphQL response in JSON. In addition, it is available in the context (`$context.result`). Thus, the response mapping template is a simple passthrough of data, realized by the following predefined mapping function:

```
$utils.toJson($context.result)
```

6.3.1.5 Query

To search DynamoDB for items matching a number of criteria, one uses a DynamoDB `Query`.

Query Request The DynamoDB `Query` request looks as follows:

```
{
        "version" : "2017-02-28",
        "operation" : "Query",
        "query" {
                "expression" : "some expression",
                "expressionNames" : {
```

```
                    "#foo" : "foo"
            },
            "expressionValues" : {
                    ":bar" :  ... typed value
            }
    }
    "index" : "fooIndex",
    "nextToken" : "a pagination token",
    "limit" : 10,
    "scanIndexForward" : true,
    "consistentRead" : false,
    "select" : "ALL_ATTRIBUTES",
    "filter" : {
            ...
    }
}
```

The fields of a `Query` request are defined by DynamoDB as follows:

version The DynamoDB version. As a value, only 2017-02-28 is supported. Required.

operation The DynamoDB operation. For a Query operation set the value to Query. Required.

query The condition of the items to be retrieved from DynamoDB. Consists of expression, expressionNames and expression-Values. Required.

> **expression** The query expression, which may contain variables. Required.
>
> **expressionNames** The substitutions for names, as a list of key-value pairs. The key is the name of a variable used in the expression, the value is an attribute name of the item in DynamoDB. Optional.
>
> **expressionValues** The substitutions for values, as a list of key-value pairs. The key is the name of a variable used in the expression, the value is a literal. Optional.

filter The criteria used to filter the results from DynamoDB. Optional. Default is no filter.

112

index The index used for retrieval. Optional. Default is primary key index.

limit The max number of result entries. Optional.

scanIndexForward Flag for forward or backward query. Optional. Default is true.

consistentRead Flag for requesting consistent reads. Optional. Default is false.

nextToken The pagination token to get the next chunk (=page) of data. Optional.

select The selection of attributes to be returned. Optional. Default: the attributes projected into the index. Supported values for specifying a selection are:

> **ALL_ATTRIBUTES** Returns all attributes from the table/index.
>
> **ALL_PROJECTED_ATTRIBUTES** Returns all attributes that are projected into the index.

Query Request Mapping Template The `Query` operation of GraphQL can typically be mapped to a `Query` operation in DynamoDB. The template uses the arguments of the GraphQL query as keys for the DynamoDB Query request. The AppSync framework makes the GraphQL query arguments available in the context object. It does this automatically without us having to configure anything. It retrieves these arguments via the context object as Velocity variables.

Following is a mapping template for a GraphQL query

```
query getPosts(owner: ID!)
```

In this example, a global secondary index called `owner-index` is queried to return all posts owned by the specified ID.

```
{
        "version" : "2017-02-28",
        "operation" : "Query",
        "query" {
                "expression" : "ownerId = :ownerId",
                "expressionValues" : {
                        ":ownerId" : { "S" : "${context.arguments.owner}" }
                }
        }
        "index" : "owner-index"
}
```

Query Response   The results from DynamoDB are automatically converted into GraphQL and JSON primitive types and are available in the context ($context.result). The results have the following structure:

```
{
        items = [ ... ],
        nextToken = "pagination token",
        scannedCount = 10
}
```

The fields are defined as follows:

items The result of the DynamoDB query operation, as a list of DynamoDB items.

nextToken The pagination token specifying the next chunk (=page) of data. The token is encrypted and obfuscated.

scannedCount The size of the base set of data, before filters were applied.

Query Response Mapping   The item returned from DynamoDB is converted into a GraphQL response in JSON. In addition, it is available in the context ($context.result). Thus, the response mapping template is a simple passthrough of data, realized by the following predefined mapping function:

```
$utils.toJson($context.result)
```

114

6.3.1.6 Scan

Filtering all entries in a DynamoDB can be done by a DynamoDB `Scan` operation.

Scan Request   The DynamoDB `Scan` request looks as follows:

```
{
        "version" : "2017-02-28",
        "operation" : "Scan",
        "index" : "fooIndex",
        "limit" : 10,
        "consistentRead" : false,
        "nextToken" : "aPaginationToken",
        "totalSegments" : 10,
        "segment" : 1,
        "filter" : {
                ...
        }
}
```

The fields of a `Scan` request are defined by DynamoDB as follows:

version The DynamoDB version. As a value, only 2017-02-28 is supported. Required.

operation The DynamoDB operation. For a Scan operation set the value to Scan. Required.

filter The criteria used to filter the results from DynamoDB. Optional. Default is no filter.

index The index used for retrieval. Optional. Default is primary key index.

limit The max number of result entries. Optional.

consistentRead Flag for requesting consistent reads. Optional. Default is false.

nextToken The pagination token to get the next chunk (=page) of data. Optional.

select The selection of attributes to be returned. Optional. Default: the attributes projected into the index. Supported values for specifying a selection are:

ALL_ATTRIBUTES Returns all attributes from the table/index.

ALL_PROJECTED_ATTRIBUTES Returns all attributes that are projected into the index.

totalSegments The number of segments for a parallel scan. Optional.

segment The table segment for a parallel scan. Optional.

Scan Request Mapping The query operation of GraphQL can be mapped to a Scan operation in DynamoDB. The template uses the arguments of the GraphQL query as keys for the DynamoDB Scan request. The AppSync framework makes the GraphQL query arguments available in the context object. It does this automatically without us having to configure anything. It retrieves these arguments via the **context** object as Velocity variables.

Following is a mapping template for a GraphQL query

```
query postsMatching(title_search: String!)
```

The above GraphQL query is supposed to return all posts that have a title starting with the argument **title_search**. This argument is provided as input to the GraphQL query.

```
{
        "version" : "2017-02-28",
        "operation" : "Scan",
        "filter" : {
                "expression" : "begins_with(title, :title)",
                "expressionValues" : {
                        ":title" : { "S" : "${context.arguments.title_search}" }
                },
        }
}
```

116

Scan Response The results of a DynamoDB Scan have the following structure:

```
{
        items = [ ... ],
        nextToken = "pagination token",
        scannedCount = 10
}
```

The fields are defined as follows:

items The result of the DynamoDB scan operation, as a list of DynamoDB items.

nextToken The pagination token specifying the next chunk (=page) of data. The token is encrypted and obfuscated.

scannedCount The size of the base set of data, before filters were applied.

Scan Response Mapping The item returned from DynamoDB is converted into a GraphQL response in JSON. In addition, it is available in the context (`$context.result`). Thus, the response mapping template is a simple passthrough of data, realized by the following predefined mapping function:

```
$utils.toJson($context.result)
```

6.3.2 Elasticsearch Resolver Templates

The AWS AppSync resolver for Amazon Elasticsearch Service enables us to use GraphQL to store and retrieve data in existing Amazon ES domains in our account. This resolver works by allowing us to map an incoming GraphQL request into an Amazon ES request, and then map the Amazon ES response back to GraphQL. This section describes the mapping templates for the supported Amazon Elasticsearch operations.

6.3.2.1 Elasticsearch Request

Most Elasticsearch requests look the same, thus a template-based approach makes a lot of sense. The setup of the following example is an Elasticsearch domain with documents of type post, and an index on their id. In the following, we show a search in this Elasticsearch domain. It is specified in the body section of the request, and especially in the query field. To search for items by the author "Biehl", or "Biel", or both, we could use the following Elasticsearch request:

```
{
        "version":"2017-02-28",
        "operation":"GET",
        "path":"/id/post/_search",
        "params":{
                "headers":{},
                "queryString":{},
                "body": {
                        "from":0,
                        "size":50,
                        "query" : {
                                "bool" : {
                                        "should" : [
                                                {"match" : { "author" : "Biehl" }},
                                                {"match" : { "author" : "Biel" }}
                                        ]
                                }
                        }
                }
        }
}
```

In the following, we introduce the fields of an Elasticsearch request:

operation HTTP method (GET, POST, PUT, HEAD or DELETE) for accessing Elasticsearch.

path The URL for an Elasticsearch request.

params The container object for all the search parameter listed in the following.

headers The header information, as key-value pairs.

queryString The common options, as key-value pairs. An example is the code formatting for JSON responses.

118

body This is the main part of the request, allowing AWS App-
Sync to craft a well-formed search request to the Amazon
ES domain. The key must be a string comprised of an
object. A couple of demonstrations are shown below.

6.3.2.2 Request Mapping Template

The template uses the arguments of the GraphQL query as keys
for the Elasticsearch request. The AppSync framework makes
the GraphQL query arguments available in the context object. It
does this automatically without us having to configure anything.
It retrieves these arguments via the `context` object as Velocity
variables.

```
query {
        searchForState(state: "washington"){
                ...
        }
}
```

The mapping template for the above GraphQL query could
take the state as an argument:

```
"body":{
        "from":0,
        "size":50,
        "query" : {
                "multi_match" : {
                        "query" : "$context.arguments.state",
                        "fields" : ["city", "state"]
                }
        }
}
```

6.3.2.3 Response Mapping Template

Elasticsearch returns a response to AWS AppSync that needs
to be converted to JSON. The Elasticsearch response contains a
couple of fields, of which the `_source` field is most relevant. The
`_source` field may contain either an individual document or a
list of documents. For both cases, a response mapping template
is provided by AppSync:

119

List of Results The list of results can be converted to JSON as follows:

```
[
    #foreach($entry in $context.result.hits.hits)
    #if( $velocityCount > 1 ) , #end
        $utils.toJson($entry.get("_source"))
    #end
]
```

Individual Item An individual item can be converted to JSON as follows:

```
$utils.toJson($context.result.get("_source"))
```

6.3.3 Lambda Resolver Templates

AWS Lambda provides serverless functions, that can be triggered by other AWS solutions, such as AWS AppSync. The input for a lambda invocation is for example:

```
{
    "version": string,
    "operation": Invoke|BatchInvoke,
    "payload": any type
}
```

Here is the JSON schema representation for the Lambda invocation input.

```
{
    "definitions": {},
    "$schema": "http://json-schema.org/draft-06/schema#",
    "$id": "http://aws.amazon.com/appsync/request-mapping-template.json",
    "type": "object",
    "properties": {
        "version": {
            "$id": "/properties/version",
            "type": "string",
            "enum": [
                "2017-02-28"
            ],
            "title": "The Mapping template version.",
            "default": "2017-02-28"
        },
        "operation": {
            "$id": "/properties/operation",
            "type": "string",
            "enum": [
                "Invoke",
                "BatchInvoke"
```

```
        ],
        "title": "The Mapping template operation.",
        "description": "What operation to execute.",
        "default": "Invoke"
      },
      "payload": {}
    },
    "required": [
        "version",
        "operation"
    ],
    "additionalProperties": false
}
```

6.3.3.1 Request Mapping Template

The Lambda request mapping template is fairly simple. Here is an example of a template, where we chose to set the **version** value statically, the **operation** value statically to **Invoke**, the **field** value statically to **getPost**, and pass the **arguments** dynamically from the GraphQL query via **$context.arguments**.

```
{
    "version": "2017-02-28",
    "operation": "Invoke",
    "payload": {
        "field": "getPost",
        "arguments": $utils.toJson($context.arguments)
    }
}
```

For a given GraphQL query, the input is resolved. The resolved mapping document will be passed as input to the Lambda function. So for the given GraphQL query:

```
query getPost("001"){ ... }
```

The resolved input looks as follows:

```
{
    "version": "2017-02-28",
    "operation": "Invoke",
    "payload": {
        "field": "getPost",
        "arguments": {
            "id": "001"
        }
    }
}
```

The fields of a Lambda invocation request are defined as follows:

version The version. As a value, only 2017-02-28 is supported. Required.

operation The Lambda operation. Possible values are `Invoke` and `BatchInvoke`. Required.

payload A container for passing JSON to the Lambda function. Optional.

Let's study the operation parameter a little closer. Lambda supports the operations `Invoke` and `BatchInvoke`. When `Invoke` is chosen, AppSync invokes the lambda function for each request. When `BatchInvoke` is chosen, AppSync batches all requests for the current GraphQL field.

6.3.3.2 Invoke

Let's have a look at the mapping template for Invoke:

```
{
        "version": "2017-02-28",
        "operation": "Invoke",
        "payload": {
                "arguments": $utils.toJson($context.arguments)
        }
}
```

The resolved request mapping template exactly matches the input payload:

```
{
        "version": "2017-02-28",
        "operation": "Invoke",
        "payload": {
                "arguments": {
                        "id": "postId1"
                }
        }
}
```

6.3.3.3 BatchInvoke

Let's have a look at the following mapping template for Batch-Invoke:

```
{
        "version": "2017-02-28",
        "operation": "BatchInvoke",
        "payload": $utils.toJson($context)
}
```

For BatchInvoke, the mapping template is applied for every field and merged into a list. The following example template shows the merge:

```
{
        "version": "2017-02-28",
        "operation": "BatchInvoke",
        "payload": [
                {...}, // context for batch item 1
                {...}, // context for batch item 2
                {...} // context for batch item 3
        ]
}
```

The Lambda function needs to be able to process lists and is expected to produce a list as the response, such as:

```
[
        {"data":{},"errorMessage":null,"errorType":null},//result for batch item 1
        {"data":{},"errorMessage":null,"errorType":null},//result for batch item 2
        {"data":{},"errorMessage":null,"errorType":null},//result for batch item 3
]
```

6.3.3.4 Response Mapping Template

The response returned by the Lambda function is converted into a GraphQL response in JSON. It is available in the context ($context.result). Thus, the response mapping template is a simple passthrough of data, realized by the following predefined mapping function:

```
$utils.toJson($context.result)
```

If the BatchInvoke operation was used, the input to the Lambda function is a list. Symmetrically, the output of the Lambda function should also be a list, with responses in the same order and in the same quantity.

123

7 AppSync Real-Time Data & Subscriptions

7.1 What are Subscriptions

GraphQL is a *query language* for APIs. The language allows us to structure the interaction between frontend on the client and a backend on the server. The language provides primitives for specifying the data served by the API, retrieving data, writing data and getting notified when data changes. And of course, it is the later feature, getting notified by GraphQL subscriptions, that we use to realize events.

The client sends a subscription request to the GraphQL API. The client specifies in the request both the event type (in the example: `createdEvent`) to be observed and the data (fields `name`, `when`, `where` and `description`), which should be sent from the server to the client when the event is triggered.

```
subscription {
  createdEvent(where: "Zurich")  {
    name
    when
    where
    description
  }
}
```

In the above example, a client requests a subscription called `createdEvent` from the GraphQL API. The client uses this subscription to be notified whenever new events are available on the server. The client even specifies, which fields of the newly added event are relevant to be included in the notification: `name`, `when`, `where` and `description`.

125

```
type Subscription {
      createdEvent(where: String!): Event
}
```

What triggers a notification? In most cases, a notification is triggered by a modification of the data that is served by the API. This means that an event handler (for `createdEvent` in our example) needs to be installed inside the implementation of the API that modifies the event data. It will send the event to the client, when the event data changes. In rare cases, a notification could be triggered by an external event, which is not directly accessible inside the graph or only accessible in aggregated form.

The AppSync framework provides a lot of boilerplate code for event subscription. So it is fast and reliable to implement events with GraphQL. The client can influence, which fields should be delivered and which fields are not required. So the client can determine in the typical GraphQL manner, which fields it needs.

7.2 Using Subscriptions

What we have learned in chapter 5 on AppSync resolvers is mostly suited for Query and Mutation operations. Query and Mutation operations are handled in a synchronous request/response mode using the HTTP protocol.

Subscriptions, however, need to be handled differently and have different requirements for the underlying transport protocol: When a client subscribes, a long-lasting connection is established, that allows the server to push out updates in real-time. As shown before, there are two main processes in the context of subscriptions

1. Setting up a new subscription (see section 7.2.1)

2. Notification when an event occurs, via the previously set up subscription (see section 7.2.2)

126

In the following, we study how these subscriptions are supported by AppSync.

7.2.1 Subscription Setup

The first step of using GraphQL subscriptions is for the client to send a subscription request to the GraphQL API. The request specifies both the event to observe and the data, which should be sent from the server to the client, when the event is actually triggered.

```
subscription {
  createdEvent(where: "Zurich") {
    name
    when
    where
    description
  }
}
```

The observed event in the above example is `createdEvent`. It is additionally filtered, as we are only interested in being notified for events happening in `"Zurich"`. When the event is actually triggered, we want to receive the fields `name`, `when`, `where` and `description` of the newly added event.

7.2.2 Event Notification

In the following, let's talk about what happens when an event occurs. An event typically occurs when data changes. And when we stay within the GraphQL universe, data is changed exclusively by mutation operations.

AppSync supports sending a notification when a mutation operation executes. Instead of writing the corresponding code, we just add a directive in GraphQL on the respective subscription. This behavior can be configured right in the GraphQL schema, with the custom directive `@aws_subscribe`, which references the mutation operation responsible for changing the data. In our example below, a single mutation operation is referenced. But in fact, AppSync would allow us to define a list of mutation operations, such as `["createEvent","editEvent"]`.

```
type Mutation {
        createEvent(
                name: String!,
                when: String!,
                where: String!,
                description: String!
        ): Event

type Subscription {
        createdEvent(where: String!): Event
        @aws_subscribe(mutations: ["createEvent"])
}
```

The return type of the subscription (`createdEvent` in our example) must match the return type of the corresponding mutation (`createEvent` in our example): In both cases, it is the type `Event`.

7.2.3 Typical Subscription Patterns

In the previous example, the client had to provide a value of the `where` argument, when subscribing to the `createdEvent`, since `where` is defined as a mandatory argument in the GraphQL schema.

A typical pattern is to provide more than one argument and to make all of them optional, as shown in the subscription type `createdEventOpt` below. This allows the client to filter the events it wants to subscribe to, according to various filter criteria. But not all of these criteria have to be used by the client. It is even possible to subscribe without any arguments. In this case, without specifying any filter, the meaning should be to subscribe to all events.

```
type Subscription {
        createdEventOpt(where: String, when: String): Event
        @aws_subscribe(mutations: ["createEvent"])
}
```

7.3 Underlying Technology

This section is intended to provide some background information on the underlying technology, that allows us to realize subscriptions. The chosen protocol in AppSync is MQTT (see section 7.3.1) over a bidirectional Websockets channel (see section 7.3.2).

7.3.1 MQTT

MQTT stands for *Message Queue Telemetry Transport* and is standardized by ISO/IEC 20922 [7]. Technically, it is a publish-subscribe messaging protocol, so just what we need for realizing AppSync subscriptions. Since the protocol is light-weight, simple and easy to implement, it can be used in many different situations, such as for API and IoT use cases. The protocol often runs on TCP/IP, but can also run on other bidirectional protocols, such as WebSockets (see section 7.3.2). The features of MQTT include the publish-subscribe messaging pattern, one-to-many message distribution and decoupling of applications, and it is agnostic to the content of the payload. As a standard, MQTT offers three qualities of service for message delivery: "at most once", "at least once" and "exactly once". For AppSync subscriptions, the "exactly once" semantics should be used in most cases.

7.3.2 WebSockets

WebSockets is a TCP-based protocol providing a full duplex communication link between client and server [1]. WebSockets are available as an unprotected variant (`ws://`) and as a secure, TLS-protected variant (`wss://`).

WebSockets are relatively well supported by most modern browsers, and it can also be consumed by client-side JavaScript via the `WebSocket` object in modern browsers. It is also supported by modern apps and app frameworks.

The WebSocket protocol is not based on HTTP, but only on TCP, and thus some proxies or gateways won't allow it without manual configuration. There is no explicit support for events in WebSockets. However, events can just be implemented with another protocol, such as MQTT, which is sent as an application protocol on top of a bi-directional WebSockets channel.

8 AppSync API Security

We want to keep our AppSync API and the data behind it as secure as possible. We need to authenticate the API client (the app) and the end user. In addition, we need to check if both client and end user are authorized to access the API and the data it exposes. In this chapter, we first clarify the security terminology we use (see section 8.1) and then describe the security mechanisms of AppSync and AWS and how we use them (see section 8.2).

8.1 Security Foundations

Two similar terms -- authentication and authorization -- are used in the context of API security. For the following discussion, it is essential to know the distinction between the two. *Authentication* is a concept for answering the question: Who are you? Authentication is a method for providing proof of the claimed identity. *Authorization* is a concept that answers the question: What are you allowed to do? Authorization provides the rights assigned to the confirmed identity, for example, access rights. Authentication is a precondition for proper authorization.

GraphQL does not prescribe how authentication or authorization should be implemented. But best practices for implementing both authentication and authorization can be observed.

8.2 Security with AppSync

GraphQL provides several technical possibilities for securing APIs with authentication and authorization.

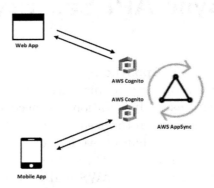

Figure 8.1: AppSync Clients and API Security

8.2.1 Security Settings

The settings page on the AppSync dashboard is the central place to configure API-specific security aspects in AppSync. There are four mechanisms to choose from:

- API-Key (see section 8.2.2)

- OpenID Connect (see section 8.2.3)

- Amazon Cognito User Pool (see section 8.2.4)

- AWS Identity and Access Management (see section 8.2.5)

Figure 8.2: Security Settings on the AppSync Dashboard

8.2.2 API Key

API keys are used to identify a client (app); an end user cannot be identified by API keys. API keys are not very secure, they are usually hardcoded in the app and could get stolen in a relatively simple manner by analyzing the app. But the handling of API keys is relatively simple. Thus API keys are often used during the development phase and for public APIs.

The API provider needs to manage a set of API keys (basically long, randomly generated strings). API keys have an expiry date. The API provider hands the API keys out to the clients.

The client attaches the API key to the HTTP header `x-api-key` for each API access.

In AppSync, the API keys are managed on the settings page of the AppSync API dashboard, shown in Figure 8.2. On this page, the API provider can create or revoke API keys.When creating an API key, the API provider can choose to set individual expiry dates.

8.2.3 OpenID Connect

OpenID Connect [3] is a standard for transporting end user identity and in its implementation, it is based on the OAuth2 framework.

In AppSync, we can use the federation capabilities of OpenID Connect. With the federation capabilities of OpenID Connect, the end user will be able to authenticate with another provider (e.g. with Google), which supports OpenID Connect, and then use the token received from that other OpenID Connect provider to call our AppSync API. If AppSync is configured for federation with a set of OpenID Connect providers, the AppSync infrastructure merely needs to checks that the token was created by one of the supported OpenID Connect providers, by checking the signature of the token.

Figure 8.3: Cognito   Security   Settings   on   the   AppSync
           Dashboard

To configure the Amazon Cognito option in AppSync, open the settings page of the AppSyncAPI dashboard shown in Figure 8.3.

- The URL of the accepted OpenID Connect provider has to be specified. This URL is used as the basis for OpenID

134

Connect discovery. With OpenID Connect discovery [11], the well-known URIs [9] and JWKS [8] it is possible to obtain the cryptographic public key, which needs to be used to check the tokens of that OpenID Connect provider.

- An optional parameter is the clientID, allowing us to limit access to tokens that were created for that application.

- Further optional parameters are used to limit the time to live of the tokens, e.g. the number of milliseconds a token is valid, after being issued for an authenticated user.

8.2.4 Amazon Cognito User Pools

Amazon Cognito is service that provides authentication, authorization, and user management capabilities for web and mobile apps. End users can sign in directly with a user name and password via the AppSync user pools. When the Amazon Cognito option is selected in AppSync, an authenticated user from a Cognito user pool is required for accessing the GraphQL API.

Figure 8.4: Cognito Security Settings on the AppSync Dashboard

To configure the Amazon Cognito option in AppSync, open

135

the settings page of the AppSyncAPI dashboard shown in Figure 8.4. We need to select the aws region and user pool. In addition, it is possible to allow or block certain apps via a regular expression on their AppID. The Amazon Cognito product and user pool needs to be set up separately, according to the Amazon Cognito documentation.

Authorization

To enforce access permissions on certain GraphQL operations based on the Cognito group (contained in the token). This is simply specified by the `@aws_auth` directive of the respective field.

```
type Query {
        posts:[Post!]!
        @aws_auth(cognito_groups: ["Bloggers", "Readers"])
}
```

Without specifying any `@aws_auth` directive or cognito user groups as parameters, a configurable default action (ALLOW or DENY) is applied.

8.2.5 AWS Identity and Access Management

With AWS IAM, clients authenticate with an AWS access key (which consists of an access key ID and secret access key) or with short-lived, temporary credentials provided by Amazon Cognito Federated Identities.

To configure the AWS IAM option in AppSync, open the settings page of the AppSyncAPI dashboard shown in Figure 8.5.

The details of the AWS Identity and Access Management need to be configured on the product and configuration page of AWS IAM. The access key and credential can be associated with an access policy as part of the AWS IAM configuration. The access policy can be managed in very fine-grained detail. An access policy may, for example, specify certain API endpoints and specific

136

Figure 8.5: AWS IAM Security Settings on the AppSync Dashboard

GraphQL methods (query, mutation, subscription) and specific fields. For further details, check the documentation for AWS IAM.

9 AppSync Clients

AppSync clients call the GraphQL API. They interact with the API using the GraphQL query language, as shown in Figure 9.1.

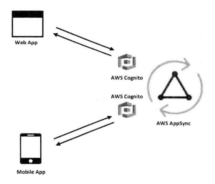

Figure 9.1: AppSync Clients

AppSync not only provides support for creating APIs but also for writing clients. Client implementations can be based on the provided app templates for iOS, Android, React Web, and React Native. An AppSync client may use the AppSync SDK, which provides advanced support for offline access, synchronization support, and conflict resolution.

In this chapter, we first give a practical introduction to writing basic AppSync clients in section 9.1, study some details of offline access and caching in section 9.2, client-side conflict resolution in section 9.3, client-side security in section 9.4 and add support for real-time data to our client in section 9.4.

9.1 Basic AppSync Clients

In this section, we build an AppSync client step-by-step. First, we define a simple API in section 9.1.1 and a simple client skeleton without API access in section 9.1.2. We continue to evolve this client, first by adding AppSync support in section 9.1.3, then by adding predefined GraphQL operations in section 9.1.4 and registering those operations in section 9.1.5. We finalize the configuration of the AppSync client in section 9.1.6 and test the client in section 9.1.7.

9.1.1 Create AppSync API

Before starting with the development of the client, we need an AppSync API, that can be consumed by the client. The API is defined by the following GraphQL schema:

```
schema {
        query: Query
        mutation: Mutation
}
type Mutation {
        addPost(id: ID!, author: String!, title: String,
                content: String!, url: String!): Post!
        updatePost(id: ID!, author: String!, title: String,
                content: String, url: expectedVersion: Int!): Post!
        deletePost(id: ID!, expectedVersion: Int): Post
}
type Post {
        id: ID!
        author: String!
        title: String
        content: String
        url: String
        ups: Int
        downs: Int
        version: Int!
}
type PaginatedPosts {
        posts: [Post!]!
        nextToken: String
}
type Query {
        allPost(count: Int, nextToken: String): PaginatedPosts!
        getPost(id: ID!): Post
}
```

This schema defines a `Post` type and operations to add, get, update, and delete `Post` objects.

140

9.1.2 Create Client App without API Access

Let's start client development by creating a simple React app with a static, local array of data. Later we will extend it with a connection to AWS AppSync. We base the implementation of the app on the template app, which AppSync provides for each major platform (iOS, Android, React Web and React Native). From the AppSync API dashboard of our API (see Figure 9.2), we can download all required resources.

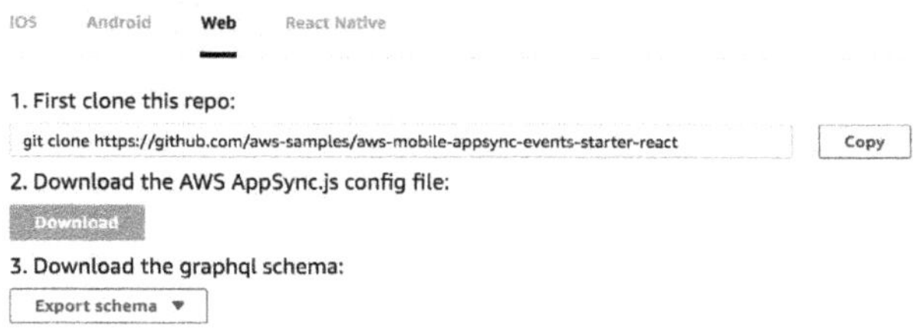

IOS   Android   **Web**   React Native
___

1. First clone this repo:

| git clone https://github.com/aws-samples/aws-mobile-appsync-events-starter-react | | Copy |

2. Download the AWS AppSync.js config file:

Download

3. Download the graphql schema:

Export schema ▼

Figure 9.2: Example Dialog for Downloading the AppSync Client Code

To create a client, let's follow these steps:

- Chose the client technology stack. AppSync supports iOS, Android, React Web and React Native. We use React Web in this example.

- We can use these templates by cloning the git repository for the respective client technology stack. For example, for the React Web template we use the following command to clone the repository.

```
git clone https://github.com/aws-samples/aws-mobile-appsync-events-starter-react
```

- Next, we install the dependencies using the npm command

```
npm install
```

141

- We download the individual AppSync config file from the provided download link and also the GraphQL schema, placing both of them into the src folder.

In addition to the code from the repository, the template app requires the following three files:

- `./src/App.js`: The main file of the app, contains two components named `AddPost` and `AllPosts`, keeps data locally.

- `./src/Components/AddPost`: A React component, displaying a form for creating a new post.

- `./src/Components/AllPosts`: A React component, listing all posts, with the possibility to edit or delete single posts.

Build and run the app as follows, and test it to be sure it works:

```
yarn && yarn start
```

We should see our project running in the browser and we should now be able to add new events. Let's add a new event and check in our DynamoDB table if the new item was, in fact, added to our database.

9.1.3 Add the AppSync API

As a preparation for attaching data from the AppSync API, we include the AWS SDK, AppSync SDK and client-side libraries for GraphQL and add the following dependencies to our app:

```
yarn add react-apollo graphql-tag aws-sdk
yarn add aws-appsync
yarn add aws-appsync-react
```

We need to get the URLs of the AppSync API from the AppSync API dashboard. Select Web/React as the platform. Download the `AppSync.js` configuration file into the local `./src` folder.

9.1.4 Add Prepared GraphQL Operations

Our client interacts with the AWS AppSync API via GraphQL queries and mutations. Each query and mutation is kept as a separate file, containing prepared templates with placeholders. Let's prepare the directory and files for the prepared GraphQL requests, as follows:

```
mkdir ./src/Queries
touch ./src/Queries/AllPostsQuery.js
touch ./src/Queries/DeletePostMutation.js
touch ./src/Queries/NewPostMutation.js
touch ./src/Queries/UpdatePostMutation.js
```

Create the file `AllPostsQuery.js` with the following contents:

```
import gql from 'graphql-tag';
export default gql`
query AllPosts {
        allPost {
                posts {
                        __typename
                        id
                        title
                        author
                        version
                }
        }
}`;
```

Create the file `DeletePostMutation.js` with the following contents:

```
import gql from 'graphql-tag';
export default gql`
mutation DeletePostMutation($id: ID!, $expectedVersion: Int!) {
        deletePost(id: $id, expectedVersion: $expectedVersion) {
                __typename
                id
                author
                title
                version
        }
}`;
```

Create the file `NewPostMutation.js` with the following contents:

```
import gql from 'graphql-tag';
export default gql`
mutation AddPostMutation($id: ID!, $author: String!, $title: String!) {
        addPost(id: $id, author: $author, title: $title, content: " ", url: " ") {
                __typename
                id
```

143

```
                author
                title
                version
        }
}`;
```

Create the file `UpdatePostMutation.js` with the following contents:

```
import gql from 'graphql-tag';
export default gql`
mutation UpdatePostMutation($id: ID!, $author: String, $title: String,
        $expectedVersion: Int!) {
        updatePost(id: $id, author: $author, title: $title,
                expectedVersion: $expectedVersion) {
                __typename
                id
                author
                title
                version
        }
}`;
```

9.1.5 Register AppSync Operations

Edit the import section of the `App.js` file, as follows:

```
import AWSAppSyncClient from "aws-appsync";
import { Rehydrated } from 'aws-appsync-react';
import { AUTH_TYPE } from "aws-appsync/lib/link/auth-link";
import { graphql, ApolloProvider, compose } from 'react-apollo';
import * as AWS from 'aws-sdk';
import AppSync from './AppSync.js';
import AllPostsQuery from './Queries/AllPostsQuery';
import NewPostMutation from './Queries/NewPostMutation';
import DeletePostMutation from './Queries/DeletePostMutation';
import UpdatePostMutation from './Queries/UpdatePostMutation';
```

Make sure the correct libraries are included and also the prepared GraphQL operations.

9.1.6 AppSync Configuration

Configure the AppSync client object from the AWS SDK by adding the following code to the file `App.js`:

```
const client = new AWSAppSyncClient({
        url: AppSync.graphqlEndpoint,
        region: AppSync.region,
        auth: {
                type: AUTH_TYPE.API_KEY,
                apiKey: AppSync.apiKey
```

144

```
        }
});
```

Replace the React component called `App` in the file `App.js`, so it looks like this:

```
class App extends Component { render() { return (
        <div className="App">
        <header className="App-header">
        <img src={logo} className="App-logo" alt="logo" />
        <h1 className="App-title">Welcome to React</h1>
        </header>
        <p className="App-intro">
        To get started, edit <code>src/App.js</code> and save to reload.
        </p>
        <NewPostWithData />
        <AllPostsWithData />
        </div>
);}}
```

Let's delete the variable `posts` in the code in file `App.js`, because the app state will be coming from AWS AppSync. At the bottom of our `App.js` file, define the following higher-order component:

```
const AllPostsWithData = compose(
        graphql(AllPostsQuery, {
                options: {
                        fetchPolicy: 'cache-and-network'
                },
                props: (props) => ({
                        posts: props.data.allPost && props.data.allPost.posts,
                })
        }),
        graphql(DeletePostMutation, {
                props: (props) => ({
                        onDelete: (post) => props.mutate({
                                variables:{id:post.id,expectedVersion:post.version},
                                optimisticResponse: () => ({
                                        deletePost: { ...post, __typename: 'Post' }
                                })
                        })
                }),
                options: {
                        refetchQueries: [{ query: AllPostsQuery }],
                        update: (proxy, { data: { deletePost: { id } } }) => {
                                const query = AllPostsQuery;
                                const data = proxy.readQuery({ query });
                                data.allPost.posts =
                                        data.allPost.posts.filter(post => post.id !== id);
                                proxy.writeQuery({ query, data });
                        }
                }
        }),
        graphql(UpdatePostMutation, {
                props: (props) => ({
                        onEdit: (post) => {
                                props.mutate({
                                        variables: {
```

145

```
                                               ...post,
                                               expectedVersion:  post.version
                                          },
                                          optimisticResponse:  () => ({ updatePost:{
                                                          ...post,
                                                          __typename:  'Post',
                                                          version:  post.version + 1
                                                 }
                                          }),
                                    })
                             }
                      }),
               options:  {
                      refetchQueries:  [{ query:  AllPostsQuery }],
                      update:  (dataProxy, { data: { updatePost } }) => {
                             const query = AllPostsQuery;
                             const data = dataProxy.readQuery({ query });
                             data.allPost.posts = data.allPost.posts.map(
                                    post =>
                                               post.id !== updatePost.id ?
                                               post : {...updatePost}
                                    );
                             dataProxy.writeQuery({ query, data });
                      }
               }
        })
)(AllPosts);
const NewPostWithData = graphql(NewPostMutation, {
        props:  (props) => ({
               onAdd:  post => props.mutate({
                      variables:  post,
                      optimisticResponse:  () => ({ addPost: {
                             ...post,
                             __typename:  'Post',
                             version:  1
                      } }),
               })
        }),
        options:  {
               refetchQueries:  [{ query:  AllPostsQuery }],
               update:  (dataProxy, { data: { addPost } }) => {
                      const query = AllPostsQuery;
                      const data = dataProxy.readQuery({ query });
                      data.allPost.posts.push(addPost);
                      dataProxy.writeQuery({ query, data });
               }
        }
})(AddPost);
```

Replace `export default App` in `App.js` with the ApolloProvider:

```
const WithProvider = () => (
        <ApolloProvider client={client}>
        <Rehydrated>
        <App />
        </Rehydrated>
        </ApolloProvider>
);
export default WithProvider;
```

9.1.7 Test

Let's test the client. We open the webpage in a browser with the command:

```
yarn start
```

In the browser app, we can now add, remove, edit, and delete data.

9.2 Client-side Offline Access

It happens less and less, but sometimes our devices need to go offline: when we happen to be in a remote area, in a tunnel or onboard an airplane. The apps we have become accustomed to require internet connectivity, but in those few cases when our device is offline temporarily, we still want to be able to use our apps. We don't just want to see a blank screen.

With an optimistic UI, data can be displayed and manipulated when the device is in an offline state. Offline support allows us to create optimistic user interfaces, that provide a consistent user experience regardless of the current availability of the network.

AppSync clients may add a local offline storage for the data delivered by the GraphQL API. This offline storage is a cache that works as follows: A copy of each query request and response is cached locally and for each mutation, the cache is updated with a write-through strategy, meaning the data is written both to the cache and to the GraphQL API.

Caching requires an identifier. In REST, HTTP caching is used and the query path is used for identifying objects. Sometimes type specific identifiers are used since they are easily available in database tables. In GraphQL the query path is not a unique identifier. The same object can be accessed using various query paths. Thus, it is preferred to use globally unique identifiers and not type specific ones for caching.

9.2.1 Offline Support with AppSync

There are important considerations that we will need to account for if we want an optimistic UI for an application, where data can be manipulated when the device is in an offline state. By default, offline support is enabled in the AWS AppSync client. If it is not wanted, it needs to be disabled explicitly with the option `disableOffline` when instantiating the client, as follows:

```
const client = new AWSAppSyncClient({
        url: AppSync.graphqlEndpoint,
        region: AppSync.region,
        auth: {
                type: AUTH_TYPE.API_KEY,
                apiKey: AppSync.apiKey,
        },
        disableOffline: true
});
```

When we need to call an AppSync API from the client, we typically use the `graphql` function to handle the details of calling the API. As part of the `graphql` function, we can configure the offline access per query, as shown below using the `fetchPolicy` option.

```
graphql(AllPostsQuery, {
        options: {
                fetchPolicy: 'cache-and-network'
        },
        props: (props) => ({
                posts: props.data.allPost && props.data.allPost.posts,
        })
});
```

The `fetchPolicy` option specifies the primary and secondary source of the data. Possible sources of the data are the network or the local in-memory cache on a platform-specific storage medium. For offline access, the `fetchPolicy` needs to be set to `cache-and-network`.

An optimistic UI does not need to wait for confirmation of a write i.e. mutation operation, before showing the result. The `optimisticResponse` option enables an optimistic UI by allowing us to pass a callback function, which is called before mutation operations. We can use this callback function to update

148

the UI before we have received a confirmation that the data we just wrote arrived on the server and the server responds with the result. The feature is handy, when in offline mode or when there is no connectivity. For example, to enable an optimistic response for adding a new object to a list, we can use the following configuration:

```
onAdd: post => props.mutate({
        variables: post,
        optimisticResponse: () => ({ addPost: {
                __typename: 'Post',
                ups: 1,
                downs: 1,
                content: '',
                url: '',
                version: 1,
                ...post
        } }),
})
```

9.3 Client-side Conflict Resolution

In AppSync, there is a client-side and a server-side component for conflict resolution. Conflict resolution is performed server-side (see section 11.2). On client-side, there is a possibility to react to any conflict decision of the server. This section describes the client-side component.

If the server determines to reject a mutation due to a conflict, it sends information about the conflict back to the client so it can run client-side conflict resolution in a callback function.

For example, we configure a mutation with a DynamoDB data source set for checking the version, and the client sent `expectedVersion:5`, as in this example:

```
graphql(UpdatePostMutation, {
        props: (props) => ({
                onEdit: (post) => {
                        props.mutate({
                                variables: { ...post, expectedVersion: 5 },
                                optimisticResponse: () => ({ updatePost: {
                                        ...post,
                                        __typename: 'Post',
                                        version: post.version + 1
                                } }),
                        })
```

```
            }
       }),
...more code
```

Let's say the data on the server is in version 7 (due to parallel updates from other clients), so the given request would fail the version check on the server. The mutation would be rejected on the server, a notification of this rejection would be sent back to the client, and a custom callback function for client-side conflict resolution would be triggered by the AppSync SDK if such a function has been registered.

9.3.1 Registering a Client-side Conflict Resolver

The client-side conflict resolver is an optional element of an AWS AppSync client. To be able to use a client-side conflict resolver, it has to be registered as a callback function in the AWS App-Sync client.

```
const client = new AWSAppSyncClient({
       url: awsconfig.ENDPOINT,
       region: awsconfig.REGION,
       auth: authInfo,
       conflictResolver,
});
```

9.3.2 Implementing a Client-side Conflict Resolver

A custom client-side conflict resolver receives the following input variables:

- mutation: GraphQL mutation statement

- mutationName: Name of a mutation is set on a GraphQL statement, Optional

- variables: Input parameters of the mutation

- data: Response from AWS AppSync of actual data in DynamoDB

150

- retries: Number of retry attempts

As output, it is expected to produce an updated mutation operation for retrying or a **DISCARD** if a retry is not required. For example, we could have the following custom callback conflict resolver:

```
const conflictResolver = ({ mutation, mutationName, variables, data, retries }) => {
        switch (mutationName) {
                case 'UpdatePostMutation':
                        return {
                                ...variables,
                                expectedVersion: data.version,
                        };
                default:
                        return false;
        }
}
```

The example checks the mutationName and adapts the mutation operation with the current version that was returned by AWS AppSync. In general, conflict resolution should be performed by AWS AppSync to avoid race conditions.

9.4 Client-Side Security

In chapter 8, we talk about the server-side security mechanisms for protecting the AppSync API. When calling this API, the corresponding client-side mechanism need to be added. The exact details depend on the choice of client-side platform and of course on the chosen server-side mechanism. The client-side security is configured on the AppSync client object by setting the appropriate type, such as

- AUTH_TYPE.API_KEY,

- AUTH_TYPE.AWS_IAM or

- AUTH_TYPE.AMAZON_COGNITO_USER_POOLS.

We can configure the client-side security in **App.js** for API-Key:

```
const client = new AWSAppSyncClient({
        url: AppSync.graphqlEndpoint,
        region: AppSync.region,
        auth: {
                type: AUTH_TYPE.API_KEY,
                apiKey: AppSync.apiKey
        }
});
```

We can configure the client-side security in **App.js** for AWS IAM:

```
const client = new AWSAppSyncClient({
        url: AppSync.graphqlEndpoint,
        region: AppSync.region,
        auth: {
                type: AUTH_TYPE.AWS_IAM,
                credentials: new AWS.Credentials({
                        accessKeyId: AWS_ACCESS_KEY_ID,
                        secretAccessKey: AWS_SECRET_ACCESS_KEY
                })
        }
});
```

We can configure the client-side security in **App.js** for Amazon Cognito Federated Identities using AWS Amplify:

```
const client = new AWSAppSyncClient({
        url: AppSync.graphqlEndpoint,
        region: AppSync.region,
        auth: {
                type: AUTH_TYPE.AWS_IAM,
                credentials: () => Auth.currentCredentials()
        }
});
```

We can configure the client-side security in **App.js** for Amazon Cognito user pools:

```
const client = new AWSAppSyncClient({
        url: AppSync.graphqlEndpoint,
        region: AppSync.region,
        auth: {
                type: AUTH_TYPE.AMAZON_COGNITO_USER_POOLS,
                jwtToken: async ()
                        => (await Auth.currentSession()).getIdToken().getJwtToken()
        }
});
```

We recommend using either IAM or Amazon Cognito user pools after onboarding with an API key. The previous code shows how to use the default configuration of AWS AppSync with an API key, referencing the **AppSync.js** file we downloaded.

9.5 Real-Time Clients

To add real-time support to our app, two steps are necessary.

- In the first step, we add a subscription capability to our API. This is done by declaring a new Subscription type in the GraphQL schema and implementing the server side subscription as described in section 7.

- In the second step, we use this subscription in our app by registering for the specific real-time change.

To follow along in this example, set up a new AppSync API with the following GraphQL schema, including a subscription type:

```
schema {
        query: Query
        mutation: Mutation
        subscription: Subscription
}
type Mutation {
        addPost(id: ID!, author: String!, title: String,
                content: String!, url: String!): Post!
        updatePost(id: ID!, author: String!, title: String,
                content: String, url: expectedVersion: Int!): Post!
        deletePost(id: ID!, expectedVersion: Int): Post
}
type Post {
        id: ID!
        author: String!
        title: String
        content: String
        url: String
        ups: Int
        downs: Int
        version: Int!
}
type PaginatedPosts {
        posts: [Post!]!
        nextToken: String
}
type Query {
        allPost(count: Int, nextToken: String): PaginatedPosts!
        getPost(id: ID!): Post
}
type Subscription {
        newPost: Post
        @aws_subscribe(mutations:["addPost"])
}
```

As we can see in the example above, the GraphQL schema has a Subscription root type, which is on the same root level as

153

Query and Mutation. The Subscription root type is a container for declaring a number of subscription types. In the example above, we declare the subscription type newPost that will deliver real-time data of type Post. To link the data with a trigger, AppSync offers the @aws_subscribe directive. It specifies the mutations that trigger the subscription, even an array of mutations can be specified. So far so good on the server-side: the API is now real-time enabled.

How are subscriptions supported on the client-side? The client needs to register for the subscription and when the subscription is triggered, it needs to be able to receive the notification and finally process the changed real-time data. The AppSync SDK and more specifically the AppSync client need to be configured. In the App.js file, edit the AllPostsWithData to include subscribeToNewPost in the props field. To propagate the real-time updates to the UI, whenever a new subscription is received, the subscription newPost needs to be passed into the option updateQuery in the file App.js.

```
const AllPostsWithData = compose(
        graphql(AllPostsQuery, {
                options: {
                        fetchPolicy: 'cache-and-network'
                },
                props: (props) => ({
                        posts: props.data.allPost && props.data.allPost.posts,
                        subscribeToNewPosts: params => {
                                props.data.subscribeToMore({
                                        document: NewPostsSubscription,
                                        updateQuery: (prev, { subscriptionData:
                                        { data : { newPost } } }) => ({
                                                ...prev,
                                                allPost: {
                                                posts: [
                                                newPost,
                                                ...prev.allPost.posts.filter(
                                                post => post.id !== newPost.id
                                                )
                                                ],
                                                __typename: 'PaginatedPosts'
                                                }
                                        })
                                });
                        }
                })
        })
);
//more code
```

154

The above example mentions the `NewPostsSubscription` document. The subscription for receiving a `newPost` Event is specified in the file `src/Queries/NewPostsSubscription.js`

```
import gql from 'graphql-tag';
export default gql`
subscription NewPostSub {
        newPost {
                __typename
                id
                title
                author
                version
        }
}`;
```

To be able to use `NewPostsSubscription` declared in the above file, add an import to `App.js`:

```
import NewPostsSubscription from './Queries/NewPostsSubscription';
```

We need to initially register to the `newPost` subscription. This is handled in `AllPosts.jsx`:

```
componentWillMount(){
        this.props.subscribeToNewPosts();
}
```

Now it is time for testing the real-time capabilities of the client. Start the client with

```
yarn start
```

When adding new Posts (e.g. via a mutation operation called from the AppSync Dashboard), we can see real-time data appearing in our app.

So far we have looked at relatively simple data objects that could be described as JSON objects in their entirety. But sometimes, data objects contain binaries, such as images or other media files. On the AWS infrastructure, we would typically store such binary files on Amazon S3. For real-time support of complex data, the AppSync SDK offers to handle the link to S3.

155

10 GraphQL - Under the Hood

All GraphQL APIs offer a number of features that we need to understand in order to build GraphQL APIs. This section teaches the mechanics behind the GraphQL features. These features are typically provided by a GraphQL runtime system and GraphQL libraries. They do not have to be coded by each API developer. However, to be able to use this predefined functionality, the libraries have to be used and configured correctly. The heart of this configuration is the GraphQL schema with its type definitions.

10.1 GraphQL Validation

Any request that is received by a GraphQL API, is first syntactically validated against the GraphQL schema. The correct usage of types, fields, arguments and other language elements is checked. In case of a validation error, a description of the error is sent back to the client. The GraphQL runtime (see section 1.2.3) typically takes on the task of request validation. The creator of the GraphQL API only needs to provide the schema.

10.2 GraphQL Execution

After the request has been validated, it needs to be interpreted and executed by the server to create a response. For the execution of the request, the GraphQL server can rely on the type system provided by the schema. The schema provides the syn-

tax, but also - at least on the top level - the semantics of a
GraphQL query. The operational semantics of the schema is
provided by the resolver function (see section 10.2.2)

At the top level of every GraphQL schema is a type that
represents all of the possible entry points into the GraphQL
API, it's often called the root type or the method (see section
3.2.4). The execution semantics depends on the method that
is executed: `query` (see section 10.2.1), `mutation` (see section
10.2.3) or `subscription` (see section 10.2.4).

10.2.1 Execution of Queries

After being validated, a GraphQL query is executed by a GraphQL
server. The GraphQL server returns a result that structurally
mirrors the shape of the requested query. Before being sent
to the client, the server serializes the result, typically in JSON
format.

Creating a response to a query is actually a traversal of the
graph. This traversal is also called resolution and is described
below. While the data on the server forms a graph structure,
the query produces a forest data structure as a result. A forest
data structure consists of one or more tree data structures. All
trees of the result forest are collected in a `data` object. This
data object forms the root of the response, which is typically
serialized in JSON. The shape of the result mirrors the shape of
the query. GraphQL queries are processed immediately and in
parallel with other queries.

The actual processing happens in the resolver function, which
we discuss in the next section. It is the task of the GraphQL
API developer to provide the resolver function.

10.2.2 Resolver Functions

The resolver function defines the operational semantics -- or behavior – of the types and fields in the schema. Each type defined in the schema needs to be backed by a resolver function. As input, the resolver function takes basically the data, which is a subgraph of the big GraphQL graph. As output, the resolver function produces either a list of matched subgraphs or a list of scalar values. Initially, the argument of the resolver function is the complete graph.

For execution, the resolver function is called recursively i.e. for each of the subgraphs produced as output. A subgraph is an instance of a certain type. When such a subgraph is processed, the resolver function of its corresponding type is called. If the resolver function for a certain subgraph produces a scalar value like a string or number, then the recursion terminates in that branch. If the resolver function for a certain subgraph produces another subgraph, the resolver function is called for each subgraph. This continues until all subgraphs are resolved to scalar values. A resolver function typically accesses a database and then constructs a response based on the result of the database query.

Previously I stated that the resolver function takes the subgraph as input. This is actually a simplification. In fact, a resolver function receives three arguments:

- `obj`: the parent object of the field being resolved (for a field of the `Query/Mutation/Subscription` type, `obj` is often `null` or left out).

- `args`: the arguments (see section 3.3.3.3) provided to the field in the GraphQL query/mutation/subscription.

- `context`: holds important contextual information, such as the authenticated user and access to a database.

10.2.3 Execution of Mutations

Executing a mutation and creating a response entails a modification of the graph. Modification may mean changing existing nodes and relations or adding new nodes and relations to the graph. In addition, the new or modified node is returned.

Mutations need to be processed sequentially to prevent race conditions. Thus, mutations are put into a queue in the order they are received. If a mutation is fired before the previous mutation has finished processing, the second mutation is put into a queue, where it waits until the first one has finished. Only then it is scheduled for processing.

Conceptually, queries are used for reading data and mutations are used for writing data. However, there is no enforcement of this rule, we could write data in a query. The only difference between mutations and queries is that queries are executed immediately and in parallel, whereas mutations are executed sequentially, in the order given. Mutation number two has to wait until mutation number one has finished.

10.2.4 Execution of Subscriptions

Handling a subscription entails registering the client for the chosen event. There is no confirmation response. A response is only generated when the event actually occurs. GraphQL does not prescribe any technology binding. It is, however, best practice to realize this bidirectional communication via the WebSocket protocol.

10.3 GraphQL Introspection

GraphQL offers an introspection feature, based on the type definitions. Introspection allows us to ask GraphQL for any information that is part of the user-defined schema at runtime.

The introspection feature does not have to be implemented by the API developer. It is provided automatically by the GraphQL runtime. The only thing that needs to be provided by the GraphQL developer are the type definitions in the schema.

There are special keywords for requesting meta information. They start with __, such as __schema or __type or __field. Here is a sample request listing all the types available, including built-in types, meta types, user-defined types and scalar types.

```
{
  __schema{
    types{
      name
    }
  }
}
```

To interact with the introspection system, no special tool is required, any GraphQL client that can execute queries, can also use the introspection capabilities.

10.4 Protocol Binding and Data Format

GraphQL is used for building distributed systems, so we need to talk about how data is sent from a client to a server and back. Which protocols are involved and how is the data serialized?

Typically, we would use a GraphQL runtime, which handles the protocol binding, serialization, and deserialization. The requests and responses are bound to the HTTP protocol and the JSON data format is used for serialization. We study how to bind requests in section 10.4.1 and how to bind responses in section 10.4.2.

10.4.1 HTTP Request Binding

On the server-side, there is a single generic HTTP endpoint (/graphql) that receives the various GraphQL requests that

161

clients send to the server. A GraphQL request that is sent to the GraphQL endpoint consists of the following components:

- the query/mutation/subscription, written in the GraphQL query language (see chapter 3.3).

- the list of variables

- the name of the operation

A GraphQL request can be mapped to an HTTP request with JSON data structures in two ways: (1) In the form of an HTTP GET with query parameters, as shown in section 10.4.1.1, or (2) in the form of an HTTP POST with a JSON document, as shown in section 10.4.1.2.

10.4.1.1 HTTP GET Request Binding

If the request is bound to an HTTP GET method, query parameters are used to encode the GraphQL query, variables, and operation name. The query is simply an expression in the GraphQL query language. The operation name is a simple string. The variables are a JSON object, which contains key-value pairs for variable-name and variable-value. This object is serialized according to JSON serialization rules. The result looks as follows.

```
HTTP GET /graphql
?query={customers{name}}
&operationName=op
&variables"={"var1":"val1","var2":"val2}
```

10.4.1.2 HTTP POST Request Binding

If the request is bound to an HTTP POST, a JSON document is used to encode the GraphQL query, variables, and operation name. Note that everything is serialized according to JSON rules, except for the value of the query field. It is a string, and

this string is serialized according to the rules of the GraphQL
query language. The result looks as follows.

```
HTTP POST /graphql
Content-Type: application/json
{""
  query: "{customers{name"}},""
  operationName: ""op,""
  variables: {""
    var1":"val1,""
    var2":"val2
  }
}
```

10.4.2 HTTP Response Binding

GraphQL responses are mapped to HTTP responses with a
JSON payload, whether the response returns an error or actual data. When actual data is returned, the payload is a JSON
object with the name **data** on the top-level. This object contains
the objects and attributes that were requested in the query/mu-
tation/subscription.

```
HTTP 200 OK
Content-Type: application/json
{
  "data": {""
    customers:[
      {""
        name":"Joe
      },
      {""
        name":"Bill
      }
    ]
  }
}
```

When processing the GraphQL request fails, a list of errors is
returned. Each error is detailed with further information, such
as a message containing more detail.

```
HTTP 200 OK
Content-Type: application/json
{"
  errors": [
    {""
      message: "An error "occurred
    }
  ]
}
```

10.5 GraphiQL

GraphiQL is a GraphQL client, which provides a simple user interface of the GraphQL API. GraphiQL is realized as a web application, and in practice, it is often hosted on the same server that runs the GraphQL API. GraphiQL is targeted at the developers of the GraphQL API and at developers building applications with the GraphQL API. It provides great support for developing GraphQL queries for clients, for testing the implementation of the GraphQL API or for a quick and simple demo of the API.

The GraphiQL tool offers syntax-directed editing, syntax highlighting and auto-completion since it is enabled by GraphQL introspection (see section 10.3). It can be used as part of an API portal where it may serve as an interactive documentation and an API discovery and exploration tool. The documentation displayed in GraphiQL is guaranteed to be consistent with the implementation since it is based on the same schema as the implementation.

11 AppSync Features

AppSync offers solutions to some of the technical challenges faced by most mobile and web application developers. Some of these solutions are part of AppSync itself, others are provided by tightly and seamlessly integrated AWS technologies that inter-operate well with AppSync. Examples of the technical challenges addressed by AppSync:

- Authentication & user management: The identity and access management of AWS and all related offerings, such as the integrated AWS Cognito provide the basis for this feature (see chapter 8).

- Offline data access: The AppSync SDK for building App-Sync clients (see chapter 9) provides libraries for managing a client-side local cache in the app and support offline scenarios (see section 9.2).

- Data synchronization between devices: With AppSync the data is kept centrally on the server. The data is easily accessible via a GraphQL API (see chapter 3) from all devices. The AppSync SDK provides libraries for conflict detection and resolution – a necessary aspect of synchronization (see section 9.3).

- Real-time data streams: AppSync subscriptions can be used to process data in near-real-time (see chapter 7).

- Cloud data conflict detection and resolution: The App-Sync SDK provide libraries for conflict detection and resolution. It can be used to manage the local cache in the app and support offline scenarios (see section 11.2).

- Logging and monitoring: As Appsync is well-integrated in the AWS landscape, it uses the AWS infrastructure for logging and monitoring, namely AWS CloudWatch, as described in section 11.4.

- Support for continuous deployments: The interactions for designing and developing AppSync solutions has been based on interactions with the user interface. But there is also a machine interface that can be used for automation, as shown in section 11.3.

11.1 Server-side Caching

At various points between client and server, caching can be performed to improve latency. Typically caching is done on the client-side (discussed in detail in section 9.2), but it can also be performed in the GraphQL resolver for accessing data on a potentially slow backend system. This last use case is considered in this section.

GraphQL could be inefficient with respect to its connection to the backend. This is due to the structure of the resolver. The structure of the resolver allows for writing clean code on the server, where every field on every type has a dedicated function for resolving the respective value. A naive implementation of this clean concept would result in a rather inefficient implementation with a database access for each field.

AppSync optimizes backend requests under the hood. It may batch of multiple backend requests and caches the responses for all fields of the object. Appsync functionality is similar to the *dataloader library* published by Facebook.

11.2 Server-side Conflict Resolution

Data conflicts occur when several clients attempt to write data at the same time or when resynchronizing after data has been edited in offline mode.

There is a client-side and a server-side component for conflict resolution. In AppSync, conflict resolution is in principle performed on server-side. On client-side, there is only the option to react to any conflict decision of the server (see section 9.3). This section describes the server-side component.

Conflict resolution is only concerned with writing access to the data, i.e. GraphQL mutations. The first part of conflict resolution is, in fact, conflict detection. So for conflict detection, Appsync asks the client, which is invoking a GraphQL mutation, to supply a version number for the data expected on the server. This version number is transmitted in the field `expectedVersion`. AWS AppSync checks for the actual version number on the server before writing to the data source.

The second part is reacting to the detected conflict. Conflict resolution basically determines if a requested write operation needs to be rejected. Based on the conflict detection it would already be possible for the server to make an automatic conflict resolution, and send a rejection decision if anything but the expected version is found on the server. But it may also let the client overrule the automatic conflict resolution. If this feature is desired, AppSync allows the client to make the final decision. To realize this behavior, a callback is performed for client-side conflict resolution (9.3).

11.3 Continuous Deployment and Automation

So far we have configured AppSync via the web interface. But this is, in fact, not the only way. AppSync can also be configured via a configuration file that is deployed on the command line interface (CLI). All we need to be able to use this feature, is install the Serverless CLI (https://serverless.com) and the Serverless AppSync Plugin (https://github.com/sid88in/serverless-appsync-plugin). With this plugin, we can deploy AppSync components via the Serverless CLI and automate the deployment, e.g. in a continuous integration tool. Serverless AppSync Plugin allows us to configure all aspects of AppSync as a configuration in the file serverless.yml.

11.4 Logging and Monitoring

For logging, monitoring and debugging of AWS AppSync requests, we use Amazon CloudWatch. In this section, we will set up a role for logging and monitoring on CloudWatch (section 11.4.1), then we setup a connection between AppSync and CloudWatch with our newly defined role (section 11.4.2), we then define monitoring of critical events (section 11.4.3) and logging with an appropriate level of detail (section 11.4.4).

11.4.1 Define AppSync Logging Permissions

AppSync needs to have the permissions to write logs to CloudWatch on our account. To configure these permissions, we open the AWS IAM console and create a new policy with the name *AWSAppSyncPushToCloudWatchLogsPolicy* and the following definition:

```
{
        "Version": "2012-10-17",
        "Statement": [
                {
                        "Effect": "Allow",
                        "Action": [
                                "logs:CreateLogGroup",
                                "logs:CreateLogStream",
                                "logs:PutLogEvents"
                        ],
                        "Resource": "*"
                }
```

```
        ]
}
```

Now we create a new role with the name *AWSAppSyncPush-ToCloudWatchLogsRole*, and attach the above policy to this role. The trust relationship of this role should be:

```
{
        "Version": "2012-10-17",
        "Statement": [
                {
                        "Effect": "Allow",
                        "Principal": {
                                "Service": "appsync.amazonaws.com"
                        },
                        "Action": "sts:AssumeRole"
                }
        ]
}
```

Copy the role ARN for the next step, where we register this role with AWS AppSync to enable writing into CloudWatch.

11.4.2 Setup CloudWatch Connection

Enable logging on an AppSync API via the settings page on the AWS AppSync dashboard.

- In the Logging section, move the slider to enable the logs.

- Provide the previously created CloudWatch ARN role.

- Configure the field resolver log level from the list.

- Save the configuration.

11.4.3 Monitoring

Once CloudWatch is set up, it provides real-time metrics. We can define triggers based on these metrics. Relevant metrics are:

- The number of client-side errors (4XX)

- The number of server-side errors (5XX)

- Latency, defined as the time between AWS AppSync receiving the request from the client and returning the response to the client.

11.4.4 Logging

Logs should provide an appropriate level of detail. If logs provide too little detail, they may not contain the critical information for resolving an issue. If logs provide too much detail, they are unreadable, may use a lot of computing and storage resources and may increase the latency of the API.

To provide an appropriate level of detail in the logs for many situations, the logging in AppSync operates on two levels: fine-grained on field-level (see section 11.4.4.1) and more coarse-grained on request-level (see section 11.4.4.2).

11.4.4.1 Field-Level Logging

Field-level logging is pretty fine-granular and captures:

- The generated request mapping including the source and arguments for each field

- The transformed response mapping for each field, which includes the data as a result of resolving that field

- Tracing information for each field

Field-level logging is configured by setting the appropriate log level. The following log levels are available:

- NONE: No field-level logs are captured.

- ERROR: Logs are only produced for fields that produce an error. The log entries contain:
  - The error section in the server response

- Field-level errors
- The generated request/response functions that got resolved for error fields

- ALL: Logs are produced for all fields in the query. The log entries contain:
  - Field-level tracing information
  - The generated request and response functions that got resolved for each field

11.4.4.2 Request-Level Logging

Request level logging is more coarse-granular and captures:

- The HTTP headers of request and response

- The GraphQL query that is being executed in the request

- The overall execution summary

- New and existing GraphQL subscriptions that are registered

Appendix

Feedback

If you enjoyed this book and got some value from it, it would be great if you could share with others what you liked about the book on the Amazon review page.

If you feel something was missing or you are not satisfied with your purchase, please contact me at matt@api-university.com. I read this email personally and am very interested in your feedback.

About the Author

Matthias has provided expertise to international and national companies on software architecture, software development processes, and software integration. At some point, he got a PhD.

Nowadays, Matthias uses his background in software engineering to help companies to realize their digital transformation agenda and to bring innovative software solutions to the market.

He also loves sharing his knowledge in the classroom, at workshops, and in his books. Matthias is an instructor at the API-University, publishes a blog on APIs, is the author of several books on APIs and regularly speaks at technology conferences.

Other Products by the Author

Book on REST & GraphQL

What is the right way to build a cool new API? For a long time, REST was thought to be the only appropriate tool for building modern APIs. But in recent years, another tool was added to the toolbox, when Facebook published GraphQL, the philosophy, and framework powering its popular API. More and more tech companies tried GraphQL and adopted it as one of their philosophies for API design. Some built GraphQL API next to their existing REST API, some replaced their REST API with GraphQL, and even others ignored the GraphQL trend to focus only on their REST API. But, not only the tech companies are divided. Following the discussions around REST and GraphQL, there seem to be two camps of gurus leading very emotional discussions.

The intention of this book is to clear up the confusion and enable us to make our own decision. For our own API. By having the necessary criteria and background info, we can choose if the hammer or the screwdriver is better for our API project. This book will not say: use the hammer or use the screwdriver. Instead, this book will enable us to make a smart, reasonable and case-specific decision, a decision tailored to the specific API we are designing.

Title: REST & GraphQL - A Discussion on API Design
Author: Matthias Biehl
Release Date: 2018
Length: ca. 100 pages
ISBN-13: 978-1717109378
https://api-university.com/books/rest-graphql

Book on RESTful API Design

Looking for Best Practices in RESTful APIs?

This book is for you! Why? Because this book is packed with best practices on many technical aspects of RESTful API Design, such as the correct use of resources, URIs, representations, content types, data formats, parameters, HTTP status codes and HTTP methods.

You want to design and develop APIs like a Pro? Use API description languages to both design APIs and develop APIs efficiently. The book introduces the two most common API description languages RAML and OpenAPI/Swagger.

Your APIs connect to legacy systems? The book shows best practices for connecting APIs to existing backend systems.

You expect lots of traffic on your API? The book shows you how to achieve high security, performance, availability and smooth evolution and versioning.

Your company cares about its customers? Learn a customer-centric design and development approach for APIs, so you can design APIs as digital products.

Title: RESTful API Design
Author: Matthias Biehl
Release Date: 2016-08-30
Length: 290 pages
ISBN-13: 978-1514735169
https://api-university.com/books/api-design

Book on Webhooks

Got RESTful APIs? Great. API consumers love them. But today, such RESTful APIs are not enough for the evolving expectations of API consumers. Their apps need to be responsive, event-based and react to changes in near real-time.

This results in a new set of requirements for the APIs, which power the apps. APIs now need to provide concepts such as events, notifications, triggers, and subscriptions. These concepts are not natively supported by the REST architectural style.

The good thing: we can engineer RESTful APIs that support events with a webhook infrastructure. The bad thing: it requires some heavy lifting. The webhook infrastructure needs to be developer-friendly, easy to use, reliable, secure and highly available.

With the best practices and design templates provided in this book, we want to help you extend your API portfolio with a modern webhook infrastructure. So you can offer both APIs and events that developers love to use.

Title: Webhooks - Events for RESTful APIs

Author: Matthias Biehl

Release Date: 2017-12-22

Length: 130 pages

ISBN-13: 978-1979717069

https://api-university.com/books/webhooks

Book on API Architecture

Looking for the big picture of building APIs? This book is for you!

Building APIs that consumers love should certainly be the goal of any API initiative. However, it is easier said than done. It requires getting the architecture for your APIs right. This book equips you with both foundations and best practices for API architecture. This book presents best practices for putting an infrastructure in place that enables efficient development of APIs. This book is for you if you want to understand the big picture of API design and development, you want to define an API architecture, establish a platform for APIs or simply want to build APIs your consumers love. What is API architecture? Architecture spans the bigger picture of APIs and can be seen from several perspectives: The architecture of the complete solution, the technical architecture of the API platform, the architecture of the API portfolio, the design decisions for a particular API proxy. This book covers all of the above perspectives on API architecture. However, to become useful, the architecture needs to be put into practice. This is why this book covers an API methodology for design and development. An API methodology provides practical guidelines for putting API architecture into practice. It explains how to develop an API architecture into an API that consumers love.

Title: API Architecture

Author: Matthias Biehl

Release Date: 2015-05-22

Length: 190 pages

ISBN-13: 978-1508676645

https://api-university.com/books/api-architecture

Book on OpenID Connect

What is the difference between OAuth 2 and OpenID Connect?

For API security there are two standards — and they both start with O. So it is no wonder, people ask all the time what the difference between the two is.

If you have read the OAuth 2 Book, you already know a lot about OAuth. The OAuth standard ensures that there is no unintended leakage of information about the resource owner to the client. For example, it is ensured that the client does not get hold of the resource owner's credentials. The OAuth standard ensures the privacy of the resource owner. However, there are cases, where the client should have the possibility to get access to specific profile information of the resource owner.

Title: OpenID Connect - Identity Layer for you API

Author: Matthias Biehl

Release Date: 2018-05-30

Length: 90 pages

ISBN-13: 978-1979718479

https://api-university.com/books/openid-connect

Book on OAuth 2.0

This book offers an introduction to API Security with OAuth 2.0. In less than 80 pages you will gain an overview of the capabilities of OAuth. You will learn the core concepts of OAuth. You will get to know all 4 OAuth Flows that are used in cloud solutions and mobile apps. If you have tried to read the official OAuth specification, you may get the impression that OAuth is complicated. This book explains OAuth in simple terms. The different OAuth Flows are visualized graphically using sequence diagrams. The diagrams allow you to see the big picture of the various OAuth interactions. This high-level overview is complemented with a rich set of example requests and responses and an explanation of the technical details. In the book, the challenges and benefits of OAuth are presented, followed by an explanation of the technical concepts of OAuth. The technical concepts include the actors, endpoints, tokens and the four OAuth flows. Each flow is described in detail, including the use cases for each flow. Extensions of OAuth - so-called profiles - are presented, such as OpenID Connect and the SAML2 Bearer Profile. Sequence diagrams are presented to explain the necessary interactions.

Title: OAuth 2.0 - Getting Started in Web-API Security

Author: Matthias Biehl

Release Date: 2014-11-15

Length: 76 pages

ISBN-13: 978-1507800911

https://api-university.com/books/oauth-2-0-book

Online Course on OAuth 2.0

Securing APIs is complicated? This course offers an introduction to API Security with OAuth 2.0. In 3 hours you will gain an overview of the capabilities of OAuth. You will learn the core concepts of OAuth. You will get to know all 4 OAuth flows that are used in cloud solutions and mobile apps. You will also be able to look over the shoulder of an expert using OAuth for the APIs of Facebook, LinkedIn, Google and Paypal.

 Title: OAuth 2.0 - Getting Started in Web-API Security

Lecturer: Matthias Biehl

Release Date: 2015-07-30

Material: Video, Workbooks, Quizzes

Length: 4h

https://api-university.com/courses/oauth-2-0-course

Online Course on RESTful API Design

Looking for best practices of RESTful API Design? This course is for you! Why? This course provides interactive video tutorials on the best practices of RESTful design. These best practices are based on the lessons learned from building and designing APIs over many years.

The course also includes video lectures on technical aspects of RESTful API Design, including the correct use of resources, URIs, representations, content-types, data formats, parameters, HTTP status codes and HTTP methods. And thanks to many interactive quizzes, learning REST becomes an engaging and exciting game-like experience.

We focus on the practical application of the knowledge, to get you ready for your first RESTful API project. The course includes guided mini-projects to get you ready for the practical application of REST.

After completing this course, you will be able to design RESTful APIs – but not just any APIs, you have all the knowledge to design APIs, which your consumers will love.

Title: RESTful API Design

Lecturer: Matthias Biehl

Release Date: 2018-05-01

Material: Video, Workbooks, Quizzes

Length: 3h

https://api-university.com/courses/restful-api-design-course

Bibliography

[1] The WebSocket API. Technical report, W3C, September 2012. 7.3.2

[2] Matthias Biehl. *RESTful API Design: Best Practices in API Design with REST (API-University Series Book 3)*. 1 edition, August 2016. 3.4.2.2

[3] Matthias Biehl. *OpenID Connect*, volume 6 of *API-University Series*. December 2017. 8.2.3

[4] Matthias Biehl. *Webhooks - Events for REST APIs*, volume 4 of *API-University Series*. December 2017. 3.3.5

[5] Matthias Biehl. *REST and GraphQL - A Discussion on API Design*, volume 7 of *API-University Series*. 2018. 3.1.3

[6] Lee Byron. GraphQL specification. Technical report, Facebook, October 2016. 1.2

[7] Henry Cuschieri. ISO/IEC 20922 message queuing telemetry transport (MQTT). Technical report, 2016. 7.3.1

[8] Michael Jones. JSON web key (JWK). Technical Report 7517, RFC Editor, Fremont, CA, USA, May 2015. 8.2.3

[9] M. Nottingham and E. Hammer-Lahav. Defining Well-Known uniform resource identifiers (URIs). Technical report, Internet Engineering Task Force (IETF), 2010. 8.2.3

[10] Velocity Project. *Velocity User Guide*. Apache, 2018. 6.1

[11] N. Sakimura, J. Bradley, M. Jones, and E. Jay. OpenID connect discovery 1.0. Technical report, OpenID, November 2014. 8.2.3

Index